A CONSULTANCY APPROACH FOR TRAINERS AND DEVELOPERS
SECOND EDITION

A
Consultancy
Approach
for
Trainers
and
Developers

Second Edition

Keri Phillips
and
Patricia Shaw

Gower

Published by
Gower Publishing Limited
Gower House
Croft Road
Aldershot
Hampshire GU11 3HR
England

Gower
Old Post Road
Brookfield
Vermont 05036
USA

Keri Phillips and Patricia Shaw have asserted their right under the Copyright, Designs and Patents Act 1988 to be identified as the
authors of this work.

British Library Cataloguing in Publication Data
Phillips, Keri
    A consultancy approach for trainers and developers. – 2nd
    edn.
    1. Business consultants
    I. Title II. Shaw, Patricia, 1953–
    658.4'6

ISBN 0 566 07937 2

Library of Congress Cataloging-in-Publication Data
Phillips, Keri.
    A consultancy approach for trainers and developers / Keri
Phillips, Patricia Shaw. — 2nd ed.
        p.   cm.
    Includes index.
    Rev. ed. of: A consultancy approach for trainers / Keri Phillips. Patricia Shaw.
1989.
    ISBN 0–566–07937–2 (hardback)
    1. Business consultants—Training of. I Shaw, Patricia.
II. Phillips, Keri. Consultancy approach for trainers. III. Title.
HD69.C6P47 1998
658.3'124—dc21   97–28406
                                                                        CIP

Phototypeset in 11 pt Palatino by Intype London Ltd and printed in Great Britain by Biddles Limited, Guildford.

Contents

Preface to second edition

The ideas in this book were first developed in the mid-1980s when the shift from a training to a consulting orientation in the field of management development was becoming a significant issue. Trainers from many different backgrounds were attending our programmes and workshops on consulting skills. We found ourselves counselling and advising people contemplating becoming independent consultants and working with training teams and departments who needed to make a fundamental shift of orientation to become internal consulting units.

It soon became apparent to us that when people talked about moving from training to consulting they could mean very different things. Our need to clarify the real objectives of our work with diverse organizations and with people from varied professional backgrounds led us to develop the framework on which this book is based.

A decade later a consulting perspective is widespread and the majority of professionals would see their work in the context of organization-wide learning and change, however specific the focus of their work or responsibilities might be. The addition of the word 'developers' to the title indicates the broad perspective that someone in the field must be able to grasp. The old distinction between Personnel and Training has been replaced by this idea of 'development' – personal development, team development, organization development, human resource development. The theoretical ideas and practical illustrations of consultancy in action contained in this book remain, we believe, pertinent to the professional competence of people in this field. The second edition gives us the opportunity to make some revisions to the original text and to add further material which reflects the focus each of us has taken in our own consulting practice in recent years.

The two additional chapters explore these areas of interest. First, Keri Phillips explores the issues facing groups and teams who are organizing themselves to work across the whole range of development activities, from training to consulting. Second, Patricia Shaw introduces ways of understanding the evolution of complex organizational systems that may help consultants integrate the way they think about their work, from local to global levels of change.

We would like to thank the many clients, working colleagues, fellow consultants, researchers and writers who have contributed directly and indirectly to this book, through their ideas and comments or through their influence on our own development.

Keri Phillips
Patricia Shaw
March 1997

1 Change and the trainer

This chapter offers an overview of the trends which are leading increasing numbers of trainers to become consultants, both within organizations and as independent professionals. Its aim is to help trainers broaden their understanding of the context in which this change in role is taking place. This is important for those who are committed to the change for the sake of their own personal and professional development, and who still need to convince others in the organization of the validity and relevance of their aspirations. We are also writing for those who may be struggling to come to terms with new and perhaps unwelcome demands being imposed upon them.

We start by outlining some of the changes taking place in organizations and the implications for managerial effectiveness. We then look at how the role of the trainer has evolved over the last 30 years. Finally we suggest how the role of consultant fits the management and organizational development needs of many of today's companies.

Organizational changes

It has become a truism to say that we live in times of rapid and increasing change. The Notes at the end of this chapter provide just a sample of the large numbers of books that discuss the impact of social, economic and technological change on organizations.[1,2,3,4]

Some of the main themes are:

- *Economic change:* emergence of the global economy; the interdependence of markets and finance in which the simple rules of free market enterprise no longer apply.
- *Technological change:* enormous strides in our ability to store, access, manipulate and communicate information of all kinds at great speed.
- *Social change:* a more varied workforce (no longer only the male breadwinner); more education but less traditional employment; a re-examination of the role of work and a greater consciousness of health and environmental issues.

The words which seem to describe our present and future world are complexity, interdependence and change, to which organizations have reacted in various ways. Some have responded to the changed economic pressures by slimming down and exercising tighter control over all functions, whereas others have decentralized and set up highly autonomous divisions. Microprocessing is eroding whole layers of middle management and organizations are experimenting with new, more flexible organizational structures. Companies are reflecting new needs and new values in society by, for example, introducing more flexible work patterns, funding health screening for all employees, implementing equal opportunity policies and taking greater social responsibility.

Some of the most interesting developments are taking place where organizations are grappling not just with the impact of *each* change but with the fact of *continuous* change itself. Much of the received wisdom about the successful management of organizations assumed a relatively stable environment in which many of our large bureaucratic organizations flourished. The acceptance of rapid change as the context has seen a new emphasis on flexibility and creativity – as in the emerging popularity of the following.

Being 'close to the customer'

'Customer Care'[5] programmes, such as those mounted by British Airways, many privatized utilities and major banks, are intended to educate the whole workforce towards a greater awareness and responsiveness to changing customer needs. A less visible example of the same trend is the attempt by some parts of the computer industry to involve customers in the design of new products, a step which goes beyond traditional market research by bringing the customer into the activities of the company.

Entrepreneurship and empowerment

The fostering of individual initiative in order to harness creativity within the organization[6] has progressed beyond the suggestion box to quality circles on the shop floor, where employees are actively involved in seeking out ways to improve productivity. In organizations where new products are vital for maintaining a competitive edge, such as in 3M and Hewlett-Packard,[7] individuals with bright ideas are funded to escape from and sometimes fight against the system as if they were a totally autonomous business unit. Rank Xerox go further, helping sections of their workforce to leave the parent organization and set up small businesses which sell back services or goods to their former employer.[8]

Multi-disciplinary structures

Traditional hierarchical structures are not adequate for coping with rapid change. Looked at simply an organization cannot respond quickly to changes in customer requirements if approval is needed from many different layers of authority and across rigidly separated functions. More organizations are making use of matrix management and cellular structures that encourage multiple links across divisions. Multi-disciplinary teams to see through particular projects are formed. Here ability and expertise are more important than hierarchical position.

Networking

Networking may refer to both technology and people. Knowledge is now a primary resource; desktop and laptop terminals allow access to information from sources all over the world. The capacity to exchange ideas and create meaning between all parts of an organization can promote creative problem-solving by enabling employees to type in questions to their terminal and receive help and suggestions from their colleagues. This idea of peer self-help and mutual development can be seen equally in the spread of support groups and action learning sets.[9] Here small groups of managers meet regularly to exchange ideas and pool experience in order to implement projects or find concrete solutions to management problems.

Corporate statements of purpose

The challenge for many organizations is to balance, on the one hand, greater flexibility and diversity, and fewer structural blocks to individual initiative, with, on the other hand, a strong sense of corporate identity and direction. In consequence, companies have been formulating 'mission statements' and 'codes of values' which are intended to inspire and align employees to a shared central purpose or vision.[10] Such statements often include 'hard' targets (e.g. 25 per cent of sales should be from products less than five years old) and 'soft' values (e.g. to respect the dignity and worth of individuals).

The consequences of change for managers

Change in organizations implies change in the way people manage and the skills and qualities required of them. The consequence seems to be an increase in the sheer range of competences being expected of managers.

We have asked several groups of senior (mostly male) managers attending programmes on organizational change to list the personal skills and qualities they believe are now needed for effectiveness. The following list is typical:

- Flexibility and creativity
- Entrepreneurial skills
- Vision
- Natural authority
- Diagnostic skills
- Problem-solving skills
- Leadership
- Risk-taking
- Accurate judgement
- Ability to use *all* available skills and contributions
- Teamwork
- Consulting skills
- Decision-making skills
- Self-development and self-awareness
- Coaching and counselling skills
- Ability to think strategically
- Ability to see the 'big picture'
- Interpersonal skills
- Sensitivity
- Ability to motivate
- A high pain threshold!

It is a diverse list that points to management as an increasingly demanding occupation. We have selected five priorities.

The ability to handle complexity and ambiguity

Managers need to be able to create and re-create the systems they work in and to define their own roles and tasks. To achieve this without undue stress takes what Edgar Schein has called emotional competence – the capacity to be stimulated rather than exhausted by the rate of change and to be able to bear high levels of self-responsibility without becoming paralysed.[11]

The ability to draw on the less traditional sources of power

As organizational structures flatten and cross-functional links are formed, managers can rely less on position or rank for their authority. Similarly the specialist cannot expect the depth of his or her expertise to guarantee influence. High levels of personal and consulting skills are needed.

Leadership abilities

Managing greater diversity and flexibility requires leadership which is not characterized by control but by the capacity to give shape to emerging direction, define outcomes and help weave individual efforts towards common goals. There is also increasing attention being paid to organizational cultures and the role of the manager as a creator and carrier of that culture,[12] which demands a heightened awareness of how behavioural norms are created, maintained and changed.

The ability to develop self and others

With greater emphasis on the importance of people, managers need to understand how adults learn and to be skilful in coaching, counselling and developing staff. The accent is on self-development. The only efficient way in which companies can ensure all employees learn faster than the rate of change is to make each person actively responsible for his or her own development. For example, there is increasing interest in learning organizations,[13] where managers constantly seek and share new insights and avoid compulsively leaping into instant activity.

The ability to work effectively in teams and groups

When interdependence is vital, managers need to be able to understand and participate in group dynamics to form, build and dissolve teams quickly and to move smoothly between leadership and membership roles. They also need to recognize and value individual differences and to be able to work with a variety of styles and cultures. Businesses that need quick responses to changing conditions cannot afford the sleepy pace and demotivation of stagnant committees and badly run meetings.

As a way of summarizing what we have said so far, we shall use a model originally developed by John Adams and Sabina Spencer.[14] It is based on two dimensions. That of timescale is self-explanatory. The other is centred on attention, i.e. the extent to which managers in organizations generally focus *outwards* towards external problems and constraints or look *inward* for direction, using intuition and insight. When these areas are combined, they form four basic orientations to organizational life: operate, innovate, anticipate and create. (See Figure 1.1.)

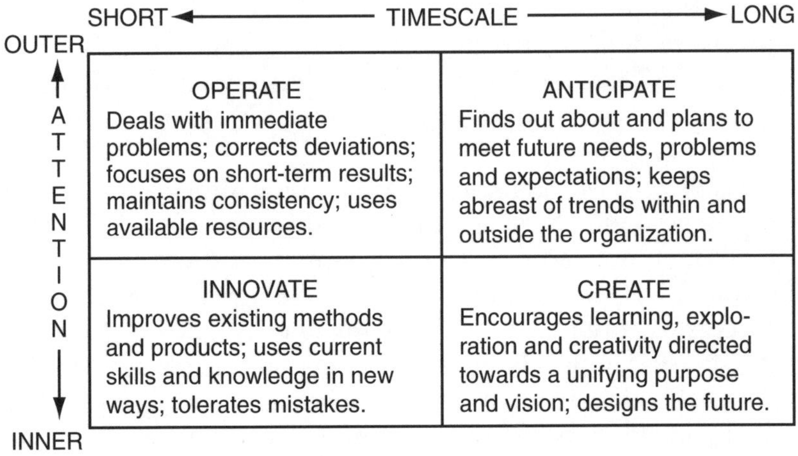

SHORT ◄————— TIMESCALE ————► LONG	
OPERATE Deals with immediate problems; corrects deviations; focuses on short-term results; maintains consistency; uses available resources.	**ANTICIPATE** Finds out about and plans to meet future needs, problems and expectations; keeps abreast of trends within and outside the organization.
INNOVATE Improves existing methods and products; uses current skills and knowledge in new ways; tolerates mistakes.	**CREATE** Encourages learning, exploration and creativity directed towards a unifying purpose and vision; designs the future.

OUTER ▲ ATTENTION ▼ INNER

Figure 1.1   Timescale/attention model

Traditionally organizations have put resources into the 'operate' and 'anticipate' quadrants. Formalized procedures and strategic planning were both efficient and effective in a relatively stable environment, but this largely analytical approach is found wanting as the rate of change accelerates. Hence a shift towards the 'innovate' and 'create' quadrants.[15] The challenge is now to create sustainability as organizations learn to function in paradoxical conditions where stability and instability must coexist.

The implications of change for trainers

The last decades have been difficult ones for traditional training and development functions. They were amongst the first casualties of cutbacks in the 1970s as organizations looked for what seemed the easiest places to reduce numbers and budgets. Redundancies were rife, Industrial Training Boards were run down, company training centres were sold, morale suffered. The late 1980s saw the emergence of a revitalized profession, born of new business imperatives. Trainers had the opportunity to become more central to organizational life, but others were in severe danger of being marginalized. During the 1990s the challenge has intensified: how to support others in coping with greater and more rapid change whilst also being in the midst of change oneself.

When the strategic resource was capital, organizations treated people as a vital but nevertheless rather uniform resource. With high premiums now being placed on innovation, creativity and communication, a company's employees really are the key to success. As organizations make greater demands of people and the necessary levels of knowledge and skill become more scarce, the development of people becomes increasingly central to the business needs of companies. The buoyancy of the profession can be witnessed in the way the number of independent consultants is multiplying; in the success of management consultancies attached to the large accountancy firms moving into the field of human resource development; and in the expansion of demand for the services of management training colleges and business schools.

Those internal training and development functions which survived the bleak times have changed or are changing; just as organizations are paying closer attention to their external environment, so training and development functions are listening even more closely to their customers. What they are hearing is likely to include some or all of the following:

- We want less delay between the identification and the meeting of development needs.
- We want development which is tailored to our different requirements rather than training courses which attempt to satisfy generalized needs.
- We want more development to take place with complete work groups and teams.
- We want more flexibility and variety in the nature of development activities.
- We want development activities which, in themselves, contribute to business results.
- We want to assess more clearly the outcomes and benefits of development activities.

As training and development functions struggle to find ways of meeting these demands, we have noticed the following trends in both the public and private sectors.

Less set menu, more à la carte
Short modules are replacing lengthy programmes. There are far fewer two- or three-week middle management programmes, for example. Instead there are more two- or three-day courses on very specific areas, and more one-day workshops, short seminars, management briefings, training updates, team-building events.

More active marketing of services
Budgeting authority in many parts of the public and private sectors is being devolved. Managers have more say in how they spend their budgets and whether to use internal or external resources. At the same time there has been a move towards training and development departments becoming profit-centres, charging for their services and competing directly with external consultancies. A marketing mentality is leading training and development functions to find out more about the needs of

potential users and to involve them more in designing development strategies. It also means that more attention is being paid to educating managers to make the best use of the function's resources.

An increase in self-development approaches

Recognizing the diversity of development needs is leading to more self-directed learning activities on courses, more use of open and distance learning methods and computer-based packages, more action learning sets and self-development groups. Support networks are encouraged to carry course learning back into the work environment. Project work is designed to do the same and there are moves to increase pre-course work by participants in order to release trainers from their didactic role on programmes. Even the use of course handouts is diminishing as participants generate their own material.

A move out of the training room

A classroom, however informal the layout, is no longer the main or only setting in which trainers work. They are to be found out and about, in managers' offices, in the boardroom, on the shop floor, using the outdoors. Even their traditional props – wall-charts, flipcharts, whiteboards, video and audio equipment – are to be found in use throughout the organization.

Just as the roles of managers have changed, becoming more varied and demanding, so the role of the trainer has expanded over the last 30 years.[16,17] When training meant fitting individuals for pre-determined job requirements, the trainer as an instructor or lecturer was perfectly adequate. When the knowledge and skills needed to perform a certain job were seen as clear-cut and consistent over time, then employees could be sent on standard courses. Training was a low-status, marginalized activity.

The impact of the behavioural sciences and humanistic values on management theory and practice in the 1950s and 1960s meant that trainers started to pay more attention to the personal development of employees. Staff and management trainers were accorded higher status than technical trainers and were expected to become more participative in their approach. Human relations and interpersonal skills training came to the fore, but trainers were still able to operate effectively in 'training laboratories' and training centres away from the mainstream of organizational life. Indeed this isolation from the normal working environment was seen as an essential condition for this type of training.

During the 1970s, when the recession started to bite, training of this sort went out of favour, and there was a return to training that could be more obviously related to the 'bottom line'. Trainers became problem-solvers in areas where lack of knowledge, poor preparation for promotion, inadequate adjustment to new organizational structures or unsatisfactory performance were hampering organizational effectiveness. Trainers needed to work more closely with managers to identify needs and to design or organize suitable courses. Trainers became part of a service function to line management along with personnel, corporate planning and IT services. By the end of the decade they were part trainer, part administrator and part internal consultant.

The shift of emphasis from training to learning has redefined the trainer's specialism. In 1985 Eugene Donnelly described a trainer as a 'manager of learning'.[18] A few years earlier the University of Lancaster introduced its MA in Management Learning, designed especially for training and development professionals. This was the first of a spate of Masters' programmes.

At the time of writing the changes we have outlined still shape the new role. Enabling others to lead and manage continuous change, with all the consequences we have described, involves the trainer as a facilitator of organizational change and development. The word 'trainer' is becoming increasingly inadequate for describing this role. Practitioners are struggling to find new labels. Charles Margerison, for example, writes of the 'active educational architect'.[19]

The role of the trainer continues to evolve into one with far greater scope and potential influence. However, with this greater scope for influence, come possibilities for confusion and self-doubt. The implications are many: for the career development of trainers whose skills and experience were gained in very different times; for the recruitment of people capable of creating and developing new roles; for the management of a function whose staff may span the range from instructor to consultant; for finding the right balance in using internal and external resources. In the following chapters we set out what we have learned about ways in which these implications can be successfully handled.

Notes

1   Robertson, J. *Future Work*, Temple Smith/Gower 1985.
2   Handy, C. *The Future of Work*, Blackwell 1985.
3   Naisbitt, J. and Aburdene, P. *Reinventing the Corporation*, Macdonald 1985.
4   Toffler, A. *The Adaptive Corporation*, Pan/Gower 1985.
5   Peters, T.J. and Waterman, R.H. *In Search of Excellence*, Harper and Row 1982.
6   Kanter, R.M. *The Change Masters*, Counterpoint 1985.
7   Pinchot III, G. 'How Intrapreneurs Innovate', *Management Today*, December 1985.
8   Judkins, P., Weston, D. and Drew, J. *Networking in Organizations – the Rank Xerox Experiment*, Gower 1985.
9   Revans, R. *Action Learning: New Techniques for Management*, Blond and Briggs 1980.
10   Adams, J.D. (ed.) *Transforming Work*, Miles River Press 1984.
11   Schein, E.H. *Career Dynamics: Matching Individual and Organization Needs*, Addison-Wesley 1978.
12   Schein, E.H. *Organizational Culture and Leadership*, Jossey-Bass 1996.
13   Garratt, B. *The Learning Organization: the Need for Directors Who Think*, Fontana/Gower 1987.
14   Adams, J. and Spencer, S. 'Why Strategic Planning Fails', *Strategic Directions*, October 1986.
15   Hurst, D.K. 'Of Boxes, Bubbles and Effective Management', *Harvard Business Review*, May–June 1984.
16   Davies, J. 'Patterns and Paradoxes of Trainers' Careers: the Implications for the Influence of Training', *Journal of European Industrial Training*, Vol. 9, No. 5, 1985.
17   Pettigrew, A.H., Jones, G. and Reason, P.W. *Organizational and Behavioural*

Aspects of the Role of the Training Officer in the UK Chemical Industry: a Research Study in Two Phases in the Chemical Industry, Chemical and Allied Products Industry Training Board 1981.

18   Donnelly, E. 'Tomorrow's Industrial Training Officer: the Challenge of Change', *Journal of European and Industrial Training,* Vol. 9, No. 5, 1985.

19   Margerison, C. 'Developing Managers', in Bennett, R. (ed.) *Improving Trainer Effectiveness,* Gower 1988.

2 Three development paths for trainers

When the label 'trainer' is given to people working in very different ways, it quickly becomes confusing to talk about the changing role of trainers. Job titles are being coined all the time; some of them are new and some of them are already in use in other fields. Rarely do these terms have shared meanings. These are just some of the phrases we have come across recently:

- Development consultant
- Learning specialist
- Educational architect
- Manager of learning.

The cynic might well raise an eyebrow at this rash of new labels, but to us their appearance is symptomatic of a struggle to redefine ways in which someone in the field of management development can work. Such redefinition seems inevitable when a role is evolving, but for the sake of clarity in this book we need to pin down the meaning of the terms we choose to use. We start by distinguishing between four ways of working, attaching a label to each one:

- Trainer
- Training consultant
- Learning consultant
- Organization change consultant.

Examining the differences between these enables us to identify three broad developmental paths for trainers:

(a)   from training to consulting
(b)   from training to learning
(c)   from individual change to organizational change.

The rest of this chapter explores these ideas in detail.

Trainer

A trainer is involved primarily in face-to-face work with groups of people on courses, seminars or workshops. The trainer uses a range of methods for giving individuals the opportunity to acquire knowledge and skills for increasing their effectiveness back at work (lectures, discussions, exercises, role-plays, case studies and simulations).

The trainer often designs and runs programmes to meet a range of *job-related needs* in the organization. Examples would be induction training for new entrants, training for first-line supervisors, equal opportunity training for all employees, interviewing skills training for managers involved in recruitment, consulting and influencing skills training for internal advisers and training in finance for non-financial managers.

Trainers may also design and run courses to meet a range of training needs which have been identified as important aspects of staff competence, whatever their specific jobs. These might include training in communication skills, assertiveness, team membership and leadership skills, creative problem-solving, presentation skills and time management.

Trainers are responsible to the training department for providing a service to the rest of the organization which contributes to its overall effectiveness. Trainers may also spend time in various administrative, supervisory and other activities associated with running a series of training courses.

Training consultant

He or she mounts a single training programme or series of training programmes tailored to meet the training needs of a particular group in the organization. Although still responsible to the training department for providing a service, the training consultant works with a sponsoring client for each project. The consultant's role is to help the client use training to deal with problems related to staff effectivness in the area for which the client is responsible.

Whereas for the trainer the training programme is the culmination and main focus of work, for the training consultant the training programme is part of the implementation stage of a consulting project. Examples might include training in team leadership skills for the project team leaders reporting to the IT services manager; the conduct of effective meetings for the trade union official and personnel manager; and communication skills for administrative staff reporting to the customer services manager at a local office.

Sometimes the sponsoring client may invite the services of the training consultant, sometimes the consultant may take the initiative in persuading a potential client he or she could help in increasing the effectiveness of the client's team, section or department. Training consultants may run the training programmes themselves or organize other internal or external resources to do this.

Learning consultant

The learning consultant also works with a sponsoring client to increase the effectiveness of that part of the organization for which the client is responsible. However, the *training consultant* designs a *linear* process whereby:

1   Situations are analysed in terms of individual and group training needs.
2   These people then attend a training programme designed to give them the opportunity to acquire the specific knowledge and skills identified.
3   These people transfer the learning to their work activities.

The *learning consultant* designs a *simultaneous* process whereby:

1   Problems are analysed in terms of individual and group development needs.
2   These people engage in activities designed to enable them to learn *through* their work.

Although this may mean that groups still attend a development programme, the learning consultant works with live issues and tasks, whereas the training consultant works mainly with simulated material.

The objective of the learning consultant is to facilitate the self- and mutual development of staff in a way that is integrated into work activities. Examples could include using a monthly project team meeting for a team-building event; helping a marketing group learn creative problem-solving techniques as they work on difficulties associated with promoting a new product; being a set adviser to an action learning group of managers; acting as a third party at an appraisal interview where both manager and subordinate are learning about feedback and joint goal-setting skills.

As with the training consultant, any development activity or event designed and facilitated by the learning consultant will be part of the implementation stage of a consulting project with a sponsoring client.

Organization change consultant

His or her work is similar to that of the learning consultant but with a different focus. Where the latter facilitates *individual* change and development in order to increase organizational effectiveness, the organization change consultant facilitates the change and development of the *whole organization*. In practice this means that the organization change consultant works as though the whole organization is the client, whichever individual manager or group she or he is collaborating with on a particular project.

In this sense the work starts to merge with that of the traditional organization development (OD)[1] consultant, but instead of a background in designing large systems change, the organization change consultant works, like the learning consultant, from a thorough understanding of the learning process.

The organization change consultant builds an extra layer into the design of development activities by *explicitly* addressing how the activity contributes to the direction of desired change in the organization. Clearly in order to be able to do this the consultant needs to be working with those who are formulating the long-term strategy and medium-term goals for the company. He or she then works with sponsoring clients to enable them to learn how to be more effective in setting and meeting departmental, section, team and individual objectives in this context.

The task of the organization change consultant is to support change by creating a learning organization where active participation in the design of change is encouraged at all levels, and where individuals learn and develop through this process. Examples could include facilitating senior management planning meetings; acting as an adviser to working parties; mediating between departments, sections, and layers of management; facilitating visioning and change workshops; and reviewing the implementation of change strategies with line managers.

Figure 2.1 summarizes and compares these four ways of working.

By way of illustration, we now introduce four case studies.

	TRAINER	TRAINING CONSULTANT	LEARNING CONSULTANT	ORGANIZATION CHANGE CONSULTANT
PRIMARY CONTRACT	With trainee on training programme	With client sponsor	With client sponsor	With whole organization through client sponsor
FOCUS OF WORK	Running training programmes	Providing tailored training	Facilitating self- and mutual development	Facilitating organizational change and development
PURPOSE UNDERSTOOD IN TERMS OF	General organizational training needs	Client's management problem and associated training needs	Issues and concerns in client's area of responsibility and associated development needs	Desired direction of organizational change and associated development needs in client's area of responsibility
IMPACT ON ORGANIZATIONAL EFFECTIVENESS	Indirect	Localized	Localized	Diffused
MATERIAL WORKED WITH	Mainly simulated	Simulated and live	Mainly live	Live
APPLICATION	Requires transfer of learning to work situation and work relationships	Requires transfer of learning to work situation	Learning and working are simultaneous	Learning and working are simultaneous

Figure 2.1   Four approaches to training and consultancy

Case 1: training

A large government department had conducted a survey of training needs amongst executive officer grades which revealed a concern about a lack of assertion and influencing skills. Although these areas formed a part of general supervisory and management training courses, the training department wanted to offer a short module specifically to address these aspects of personal effectiveness. The trainers involved in the project reviewed the training needs data and designed a workshop which would stand alone but fit into the menu of training programmes offered by the training department.

Trainees were introduced to the concept of personal power and a model of the attitudes, feelings and behaviours which support it. They engaged in a number of exercises to explore these ideas and assessed themselves against this framework.

They then undertook role-play work centred on work issues of concern to them, in order to practise the new skills and ease the application of learning back at work.

Case 2: training consultancy

A director of a private health insurance company was responsible for negotiating an employee health screening contract with a large customer organization. As well as administering a number of agreed tests, screening staff were expected to offer health education counselling to the company's employees. Although the screening staff had basic counselling skills, the client wanted to mount a specific training programme for the staff involved on the project.

The training consultants helped him to draw up the performance criteria for these staff and interviewed them to find out what difficulties they were encountering in their early work on the project. They designed a training programme in collaboration with their client, where he covered essential medical knowledge and they covered associated counselling skills and concepts. All course materials, case studies and exercises were tailored to match actual experiences with the project. The training consultants arranged to visit the staff on site some time after the training course to help with any difficulties encountered in applying the course learning, to feed back to them data collected on the impact of the screening project to date and to assess the need for further training.

Case 3: learning consultancy

A large multinational organization had moved from a structure whereby each country was responsible for the marketing and distribution of the whole product range within national boundaries to one in which cross-European product groups were responsible for different product ranges. There was concern within European headquarters that these groups were struggling with a number of blocks to their effectiveness, including communication problems, cross-cultural differences and conflicting interests between the European group and individual member countries. The role of the learning consultants was to work with the leaders of a number of these management teams to design development which would enable task achievement and learning to take place simultaneously.

The teams held regular two-day meetings and in each case one of these was extended to allow time for team development. The effectiveness of the group was added as an agenda item and the consultants were facilitators during the meeting. Before attending, the managers completed an inventory, the data from which was then used at the meeting to explore the individual differences of style and temperament each brought to the group. This led to exchanges of feedback, wants and offers which would enable each person to be most effective in this setting. As the meeting progressed, the group was encouraged to monitor how well they were implementing their agreements with each other. They broke into smaller groups to address priority areas of concern and reported back to the meeting with suggestions for improvement. They reviewed the entire meeting to extract learning about group development, effective problem-solving and decision-making. All the material generated during the meeting was typed and circulated to all members. A regular review of progress was added as an agenda item for future meetings.

Case 4: organization change consultancy

A large firm of economic planning and computer consultants had recently combined a number of divisions to form a management consulting group. The directors of this group had some clear goals for the future but strategy was still being formulated. Discussions between the organization change consultants and some of the directors revealed a number of blocks to the direction of desired change. These included:

1   An expert approach to consultancy which was the hallmark of the traditional background of the firm.
2   Sharp divisions between the disciplines within the group. Little sense of unity of purpose and standards within the new group.
3   Some disaffection amongst consultants about their own lack of development within the firm.

The aim of this assignment was to help the group develop a unified approach to consulting, improve multi-disciplinary teamwork and develop individual skills.

The consultants designed an approach whereby a selected group of staff who were seen as capable of influencing the future of the group attended a development programme. They were given reading about consulting styles, and staff from each discipline talked to the others about their work in this context. The implications for collaborative work between disciplines and with clients were explored, in terms of the stages of consultancy and in relation to current projects. Once the group had grasped the nature of the change in style, they applied the ideas to change within their own organization. They reviewed the future goals document which the managing director had talked through with them and they worked together to diagnose the blocks to change within the company.

The consultants then acted as third parties to a meeting between the staff and the directors where the staff experimented with establishing a collaborative relationship with the directors for influencing and shaping strategies for the future. This then led to a number of cross-disciplinary teams being set up to progress priority areas such as marketing the management consultancy and drawing up a code of values and working practices for the group.

These examples are intended to give a flavour of four ways of meeting the training and development needs of organizations, as we outlined them in Chapter 1. The order in which we have described them reflects a possible sequence of development for trainers. The move from trainer to training consultant to learning consultant to organization change consultant is a move along the following dimensions:

Narrower	→ ORGANIZATIONAL PERSPECTIVE →	Wider
Lesser	⟶ DEGREE OF INFLUENCE ⟶	Greater
Shorter	⟶ TIMESCALE OF PROJECTS ⟶	Longer
Single	⟶ LEVELS OF WORKING ⟶	Multiple
Reactive	⟶ ORIENTATION ⟶	Proactive

However, to suggest this is the main or only way trainers can develop would be simplistic. There will be different starting points and different goals for different individuals. For this reason, instead of writing about sequential development we have found it more useful to describe three parallel paths. Each path distinguishes a key aspect of consultant learning. We now describe each one in turn.

Development paths for trainers

The path from training to consulting

Working collaboratively with a client manager on a consulting project is not necessarily part of traditional trainers' experience; trainers need to learn about the different stages of consultancy and to develop the specific consulting skills associated with each stage. As we shall discuss more fully in Chapter 4, the traditional training cycle and the consulting cycle have many similarities at the level of tasks and procedures. Trainers who are actively involved in all aspects of the training cycle will have experiences, knowledge and skills on which they can build in developing as consultants. However, as research shows, most trainers are mainly involved in direct training, i.e. face-to-face work with groups of trainees.[2] Training needs analysis, setting training objectives, and designing and preparing training courses were also significant aspects of most trainers' work.

Involvement in other activities which could provide valuable developmental experience was less common. These included pre- and post-course individual counselling and coaching, evaluating the effectiveness of training programmes, advising people in the organization and liaising with other functions and outside agencies. Trainers with this experience will find the move to consulting easier than those without.

The approaches we describe in this book assume that the consultant's intention is to promote client learning and development, which implies collaborative work between consultant and client, rather than the consultant as expert prescribing solutions to client problems. Trainers will need to develop the personal skills necessary to form and sustain effective long-term partnerships with a wide variety of clients.

Some trainers will have experience which provides a valuable basis for development along this path, e.g. participative training in which the trainer actively engages trainees in all aspects of the programme, rather than more formal, instructional training methods. Trainers who run any kind of interpersonal skills courses will have developed many of the personal skills needed for client work. Such courses might include influencing skills, negotiating skills, communication skills and assertiveness training.

A theme to which we shall frequently return is the greater ambiguity of consulting work as compared with training. The consultant makes far more use of self than the trainer, who has many more props to hide behind (exercises, theories, lectures etc.). Trainers who have developed their self-knowledge and self-awareness have more confidence in facing the uncertainties and open-endedness of consulting work.

The path from training to learning

In this path there is a shift of responsibility for learning away from the trainer on to the learner. Trainers normally expect to identify training needs and propose training solutions themselves. A learning approach means that the learner is actively involved in defining his or her learning needs and designing ways of meeting them. The learning consultant knows how to help other people learn through self-development. To move in this direction trainers need to acquire a thorough knowledge of how adults learn and of the different preferences people have in the way they learn. They also need to be able to help managers assess their own learning styles and other factors which may facilitate or block learning. Added to this, they need to be able to design learning opportunities that contribute to work task achievement. The consultant's ability to manage relationships with clients needs to be augmented by relationship skills in the role of coach, mentor, counsellor and facilitator.

Once again some trainers will have experience that prepares them for working in this way. Those that use some self-directed learning approaches on training courses will have useful knowledge of self-development methods. Experience as a trainer or participant on unstructured training programmes and action learning sets are all very valuable, as is experience of counselling, all kinds of group work and involvement with networks and support groups. It is important to recognize that the shift from training to learning is qualitative. It requires a different orientation in order *genuinely* to deal with issues of shared responsibility.

Chapter 6 will explore this development path in more detail.

The path from individual change to organizational change

Again, reorientation is necessary. All activities must be looked at in the context of the evolution of the organization as a whole. The organization change consultant sees each project and each client relationship as a microcosm reflecting wider organizational issues. Trainers developing along this path need to widen their horizons sufficiently to see how models of individual change and development may apply on a larger scale, a leap of imagination that requires a sound grasp of systemic thinking.

In order to shift from individual to collective learning and change, the consultant needs to work at many levels simultaneously, not all of them explicit at any one time. Such consultants also require a high level of personal skill and confidence in order to use themselves as catalysts to enable others to create fresh patterns of interaction.

Trainers best placed to make this move are likely to have worked closely with people throughout the organization and with all levels of managers to the most senior. Involvement with change programmes, such as departmental restructuring, acquisitions and mergers, customer care programmes, or succession planning, may have given trainers experience of organizational change. At a personal level those trainers who have taken a very proactive approach to their own development and have sought to understand their own responses to change are most likely to tread this development path with confidence. Chapter 8 examines it in greater detail.

Figure 2.2 provides a summary of useful or necessary experience and competences acquired by trainers on each development path. Figure 2.3 combines the concepts of training and consultancy approaches with that of development paths.

Our framework then suggests that each of the consulting approaches requires progress along one, two or all three paths.

USEFUL/NECESSARY PREVIOUS EXPERIENCE	THE DEVELOPMENT PATHS	COMPETENCES ACQUIRED
Training of trainers; participative training; interpersonal skills training dealing with people's real work problems on courses; pre- and post-course briefings; involvement in all aspects of training cycle (e.g. training needs analysis, design, evaluation)	From training to consulting	Becoming more active/visible in the organization; experience in all aspects of the consulting cycle (gaining entry, contracting, data gathering, diagnosis and feedback of recommendations, implementation, follow-up); building collaborative relationships with clients; enhanced training design skills; greater business awareness
Experience of organizations and work other than as a trainer; running self-development/ self-directed activities on courses; experience of personal awareness training (as trainer or participant); experience of counselling/ therapy; running unstructured training; group-work experience; working with teams; experience of action learning/networks/ support groups	From training to learning	Recognizing training as only one way of developing people; understanding how adults learn; enabling self/mutual development; developing managers as developers of others; able to work as mentor, coach, counsellor, facilitator, as well as trainer; designing learning events which are directly productive for work tasks; identifying/creating learning resources
Proactive development of own career; thorough knowledge of own org. experience/ knowledge of different organizational forms; team-building; working with senior mgt; working with whole dept./small org.; curiosity/ interest in wider issues (e.g. social, economic, political, business trends)	From individual change to organizational change	Designing development which supports org. change taking a whole-system perspective; taking a long-term view; ability to conceptualize about complex change; facilitating organizational activities; working with all levels of management; using self as a catalyst; working with org. culture and purpose

Figure 2.2 The development paths

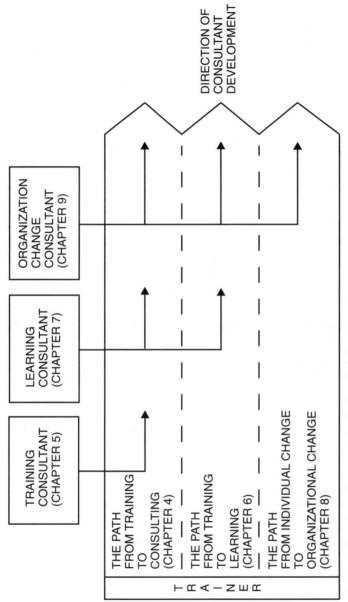

Figure 2.3   A model for trainer development

29

For example, to work as a training consultant means acquiring the skills of collaborative consultancy; to work as a learning consultant requires in addition the capacity to enable self-development; to work as an organization change consultant requires, in addition to both of these, the capacity to work with the total system.

The implications of this framework are:

1   The choice of consulting approach defines the choice of development paths.
2   The choice of consulting approach for any particular assignment depends on:
    – the client's needs and expectations,
    – the ability of the consultant to see the opportunities inherent in the situation,
    – the consultant's contracting skills, particularly in challenging the parameters of the assignment as it develops.

The framework provides a model for the rest of the book as can be seen in Figure 2.3.

We shall start in Chapter 3 by describing certain fundamental training attitudes which need to be relinquished for development along any of the paths.

Notes

1   Bennis, W.G. *Organization Development: its Nature, Origins and Prospects,* Addison-Wesley 1969.
2   Bennett, R. (ed.) *Improving Trainer Effectiveness,* Gower 1988.

3 The personal challenge

Experience as a management trainer provides an excellent basis for developing as a consultant, but it is also true that certain characteristics and approaches which contribute to success as a trainer can militate against effectiveness as a consultant. Unfortunately it is often easier to learn new ways than relinquish old ones. Many people treasure those attitudes and methods on which they have based their current sense of competence; they cling to them for support in new situations where their self-confidence seems more fragile. Sometimes the familiar skills will stand them in good stead, and in subsequent chapters we will consider the skills trainers can build on as they develop along the three paths we indicated in Chapter 2; but in this chapter we concentrate on those aspects of being a trainer which are best left behind because they are inappropriate for the different challenges of consulting work.

This process of letting go will be less or more difficult depending on individual experience and inclination. In working with a wide range of people in transition between training and consulting, we have identified some common problems in letting go:

- Letting go of performing, being the centre of attention and expecting 'applause'.
- Letting go of a clear-cut power position and control of events.
- Letting go of predictability and being well prepared for what comes next.

These three aspects of training – performing, power and predictability – are closely woven together in the relationships set up in the training room between a trainer and a group of course members. Learning to handle them successfully is part of a trainer's development and is likely to be a source of satisfaction and pleasure in the job. We look now at each in turn and consider how they may become a source of ineffectiveness in contexts other than training.

Letting go of performing

The notion of performance involves one or more people being active while others observe. An effective performer commands the attention and interest of an audience. Even when there is interaction between performer and audience, it is recognized by all as part of the performance. It is then the successful performer who is congratulated and applauded for achieving a good rapport.

Trainers develop the capacity to perform most obviously in order to give theory presentations, e.g. formal lectures using overhead slides or informal inputs made spontaneously with the help of a flipchart. After a lecture the trainer may invite questions or lead a discussion. He or she may encourage participation during a more informal theory input. Applause comes from course members in the form of comments like, 'You made that concept so interesting, I wasn't bored for a minute', or 'I really enjoyed the way you presented those ideas, you made it so easy to grasp.'

Although this way is the most obvious, we would argue that trainers perform in several other ways, as follows:

- When they engage in any activity in order to illustrate or demonstrate to course members some behaviour or skill, e.g. stepping into a role-play exercise to show a course member what a more assertive posture might look like. (Applause: 'Oh, I see what you mean. Yes, that works much better.')
- When they draw together the threads at the end of an exercise so that everything suddenly falls into place. (Applause: 'When you said that, things really began to make sense to me.')
- When they select a few moments from a closed circuit television recording that illustrate a point they have already made, e.g. the effect of closed questions in an interview. (Applause: Rueful laughter.)

Many trainers would probably recognize these examples as part of their repertoire, but in some situations trainers may be less conscious of their performing role.

The benefits of 'performing' in training, as we have defined it, are linked to traditional goals of teaching people knowledge and training them in the skills they need for effectiveness in their work. The trainer as performer seeks to keep people stimulated and interested, to encourage them to be receptive to new ideas and different ways of doing things and to get across salient points with maximum impact. Usually such trainers are well liked by course members, they enjoy their courses and find the material memorable. They will be deemed highly effective in their role, yet we are suggesting that these particular skills can be very unhelpful in many aspects of consulting, particularly when working with managers on live issues in their organizational setting. This becomes clear when we look at some other consequences of performing as a trainer:

1 *The interest of the subject matter is linked with the skill of the performer.* Course members are interested as much because the trainer 'made it interesting' as because of the relevance of the material or their own interest in it.

2   *Being a member of the audience is a passive role.* Course members expect the trainer to entertain and stimulate them.

3   *Audience participation is stage-managed by the performer.* The trainer leads discussions, briefs for syndicate work, suggests exercises in pairs or trios.

4   *Performers sometimes do not like being upstaged.* The trainer rarely takes a genuinely low profile position in the training group.

5   *Performers are sometimes seen as larger than life, the subject of the audience's idealized fantasies (they may even begin to see themselves that way).* Trainers 'know what they are talking about', 'know how to handle a training group' and if they make a mistake, use it to illustrate how to handle making mistakes!

6   *Performers want applause from the audience and use it to measure their success.* Trainers often collect feedback sheets at the end of the course. They want them to be positive, and if not, may feel downhearted and unappreciated.

7   *People remember a well-constructed performance.* Course members may well memorize material covered by a good performer-trainer. They may or may not leave with internalized learning.

Consider the case of John, a consultant, at a meeting with a group of client managers. He may be discussing the design of a training course (training consultant) or facilitating a team meeting (learning or organization change consultant). John, until recently, has been an effective trainer, who has enjoyed performing. There are aspects of this situation where John's skills and experience may not help him:

- It is not his job to win his clients' attention throughout and make things interesting for them. On the contrary, he needs to help them uncover what is of real interest, relevance and concern to them. He needs to be working with *their* data rather than his.
- He is not there to perform as a consultant while his clients watch. The more active and self-empowered his clients are,

the more successful will be the implementation of any consulting assignment.

- He is not there to stage-manage the interaction between people. He needs to be able to recognize the actual dynamics in the situation, help others to recognize this and to facilitate real contact and engagement.
- He is not the star in the production. He needs to be comfortable with many different roles, some of them low in visibility. He needs to be able to work implicitly out of the limelight, where his contribution is less obvious, as well as in the glare of centre-stage.
- He needs to demonstrate genuine, authentic behaviour rather than larger-than-life qualities. He needs to be trusted more than admired. The relation of performer to audience is essentially symbiotic, whereas consultants work towards client independence. 'We can do it without you.'
- He will probably receive less overt appreciation and applause for his contribution; perhaps some of it will not even be recognized. He will need to develop other less external ways of rewarding himself in his work.
- Since as a consultant he is not there to teach or train people but to help them learn, problem-solve and develop, his skills in helping people memorize things will not be sufficient. Providing instant understanding, making sense of everything for everyone, may not help anyone learn, least of all himself.

So when the meeting runs into difficulties, and especially when John believes that the managers are looking to him to justify his presence as a consultant, he may be tempted to intervene in ways that were appropriate for the training room. He may want to stand up, grab a pen, and talk about blocks to group effectiveness. He may want to give extensive feedback to the chair about her leadership style. These interventions may make good training points and have high impact but they may be less useful than a few brief comments designed to enable the group to continue to make progress.

Letting go of a clear-cut power position

The link between this section and the previous one is control. Performing successfully comes with a strong element of control, whereas effective consulting often means being willing to relinquish control.

We look first of all at the power that trainers have, as temporary leaders of the training group. In our experience trainers tend to play down the position power they draw on, preferring to focus on their more personal power base (skills, knowledge, personality). But if they do that, they are being wilfully blind to the control they exert over so many aspects of a training course. Perhaps they lay down conditions of eligibility for the programme, they decide the room layout to suit their purposes, they select which materials and facilities are and are not available to participants, they decide on a timetable and a sequence of activities, they may ask a person to leave a course if they believe them to be disrupting the learning of others. In comparison course members arriving on a training programme feel little or no position power, and much of their early behaviour demonstrates the power differential. Most trainers acquire far more than a theoretical understanding of the stages of group development (dependence, counter-dependence, independence, interdependence)[1] through the repeated experience of retaining power or engaging in power struggles or sharing power, depending on the objectives of the training course.

Perhaps the most vivid illustration of the trainer's power is what happens when trainers choose *not* to exercise the power of their position (by asking the course members what they want to do or by not giving answers or direction). Unless there has been considerable negotiation about power and roles, the trainer will be acting directly contrary to the expectations of course members. After all, only those with power are in a position to choose to give it up or delegate it, as when a trainer asks course members to plan and manage a day of self-directed workshop activities.

In comparison with the trainer, a consultant does not have

ready access to position power as a source of influence. Indeed most definitions of the term 'consultant' explicitly exclude the authority to control. Consultants really do have to rely on the effective use of themselves, their personal and consulting skills, in order to influence their clients. This is not to say that consultants do not deal all the time with issues of power. Peter Block suggests that concerns about control or vulnerability are the two major stumbling blocks in consultant–client relationships.[2] For this reason, we believe that those trainers who have never fully faced the realities of their own power position in the training room and understood how they use (and sometimes misuse) it, will be less able to relinquish control as consultants in order to see and handle effectively the different power issues they will face. They may at worst construe all events in the same terms as the power relationships they were familiar with in the training room.

There are two other relevant aspects to this question of letting go of well-defined power and control. One concerns territory, the other the explicit use of theory and exercises.

Trainers usually work on their own territory, whether at a training centre or training department. Even when using a hotel, trainers usually make sure they are familiar with the venue and have organized the layout of furniture before course members arrive.

The situation for consultants is quite different. They usually meet their clients on the latter's home ground. They have to gain entry and establish a role for themselves by good contracting. A trainer plays an important part in establishing the unwritten rules, but a consultant seeks to uncover and understand the norms of the client system.

Finally, one of the ways that trainers can exercise control is through the use of theory and exercises. Theory can promote understanding and exercises can provide opportunity for practice. At the same time they may also be ways in which the trainer seeks to prevent difficulties surfacing in the group because he or she feels unable to handle the issues. In such instances the theory or exercise intervention is one way a trainer can control the situation. On a training course, particularly one where relationships are short term, this can be effective and the trainer will, in any case, probably be meeting course members' expectations. But the consultant working with managers in their work context does not have these 'props' and reaching for them when conflict emerges may cloud issues and leave important organizational problems festering. It may be vital for the consultant not to 'handle' (in other words, control) the situation but to enable confusion, tension or conflict to be faced openly, without escape routes.

Letting go of predictability

There are many ways in which the trainer's life has more certainty and security built into it compared with that of the consultant. A few examples will illustrate this.

Workload
A series of training courses can be planned ahead in a logical manner, allowing time for preparation and other related activities. The workload is sequential, with a trainer running one course at a time, completing each assignment before starting the next. A consultant has to let go of this sort of certainty in order to juggle several incomplete projects simultaneously. Timescales and commitments may need to be renegotiated as projects are extended, expanded into new areas or curtailed. Diary planning has to be flexible enough to cope with change and the unexpected. Above all, the consultant needs to be able to live permanently with 'work in progress' rather than the satisfaction of a series of finished assignments.

Structure
Training courses follow a structured sequence of events that has been designed beforehand. Even when the course allows considerable flexibility with self-directed work by participants, the trainers are usually drawing on a pool of known resources and possibilities. The simulated nature of activities on structured training courses removes the unpredictability, politics and

extra intensity of emotional involvement which occur when live problems are being dealt with in the workplace. Although consultants have many opportunities to use their design skills, they will also have to work in situations where they really know no more than their clients about what will happen next.

Relationships

The trainer knows how long the relationship with trainees will last, because the length of the course, and any pre- or post-course work which has been built around it, are laid down. The relationship between consultant and client is much more variable. It may last hours or years. Also the nature of the trainer–trainee relationship is defined by the relative lack of ambiguity in the two roles. The consultant has to negotiate his or her role and the nature of the relationship with clients, within a far wider range of possibilities and mutual expectations. There will be questions such as the following. What is the structure of hierarchical relationships with which I will have to deal? Who are the different parties within the client system with whom I will need to contract? Who is the real decision-maker?

In summary we are suggesting that, in becoming consultants, trainers need to be willing to let go of a number of things they may well value:

- The pleasure of performing well in front of an audience.
- The security of a well-defined power position in the training room.
- The advantage of working on 'home' territory.
- The safeguard of being able to use theory and exercise to control situations.
- The predictability of a planned, sequenced workload.
- The relative simplicity of the trainer–trainee relationship.
- The luxury of working one step removed from the cauldron of organizational politics.

The basis of these preferences may have been learnt and subsequently reinforced from an early age. Hence relinquishing or modifying them can be quite disturbing. The trainer in becoming a consultant may feel under considerable pressure to behave in a clear, responsible and proactive way whilst actually feeling very uncertain. In seeking to cope with these contradictions the consultant may simply replicate the inconsistencies and hypocrisies of the organization she or he is there to help. This is elaborated in Chapter 10.

There is of course another side to all this. There are many trainers who see consultancy as an opportunity to let go of irksome, draining or dissatisfying aspects of their work. They would see the 'luxury' of reigning in the training room, isolated from the work context of managers, as a liability that keeps them removed from the mainstream of organizational life and prevents them from exerting greater influence for change. They would point to the strain of building short-term working relationships with group after group of trainees, rather than having the opportunity to develop long-term trust and collaboration with client managers. They would gladly forgo the sense of completion that comes from positive end-of-course feedback and a set of good action plans if they could have instead the chance to see learning being applied and its actual impact on individual, team or organizational effectiveness. Finally, they may be happy to exchange the adrenalin of performance for the excitement and challenge of seeing live work problems being confronted and resolved over time.

Notes

1   Weber, R.C. 'The Group: A Cycle from Birth to Death', in Porter, L. and Mohr, B. (eds), *Reading Book for Human Relations Training*, NTL Institute 1982.
2   Block, P. *Flawless Consulting: A Guide to Getting Your Expertise Used*, Learning Concepts 1981.

4 From training to consulting

In Chapter 2 we identified three development paths for trainers becoming consultants. Each of these expands the trainer's work in different but overlapping directions. Common to all three is the need to acquire consulting skills for managing relationships with clients. For training consultants this is the main development path.

Many excellent books on the principles of consultancy have already been written and we do not intend to cover the ground again. For the reader who would like a single reference in this area we would recommend *Flawless Consulting* by Peter Block.[1] What we propose to do in this chapter, as elsewhere in the book, is to approach consulting from the perspective of those with a background in training. In the last chapter we discussed what trainers need to leave behind in the transition to consulting; now we shall concentrate on the competences they can build on and new areas for development.

The definition that we find most useful describes a consultant as someone who is in a position to influence change but who has no direct authority to implement change initiatives. A client is any person or group whom the consultant seeks to influence.

As we argued in Chapter 3, the trainer does have a form of temporary authority over trainees in the training room although trainers vary in the degree to which they use or even acknowledge this authority. Nevertheless both trainers and consultants cannot be really effective without developing the capacity to influence through the personal qualities, expertise and skills which form their real power base.

The training cycle v. the consulting cycle

Both training and consulting can be described as systematic approaches involving a number of phases. Six of these are usually identified in the basic training cycle:

The training cycle
- Identifying training needs
- Setting training objectives
- Selecting methods of validation and evaluation
- Designing the training course
- Running the training course
- Carrying out validation and evaluation.

Readers may come across variations of the consulting cycle, but most practitioners would broadly agree with the following stages:

The consulting cycle
- Gaining entry
- Agreeing a working contract
- Data collection, analysis and diagnosis
- Formulating proposals
- Feedback to clients and decision to act
- Implementation
- Follow-up.

Both models are cycles in that information generated in the last stage may signal a return to earlier stages. It is more appropriate to identify separate, well-defined steps in the training cycle, as each stage should be completed before moving on to the next. In consultancy there is more often overlap between the stages and recycling within the cycle. Already this points to the greater ambiguity of consulting work.

Table 4.1 compares the two models. The arrows show where the training cycle has potential for preparing trainers for consulting work.

Table 4.1

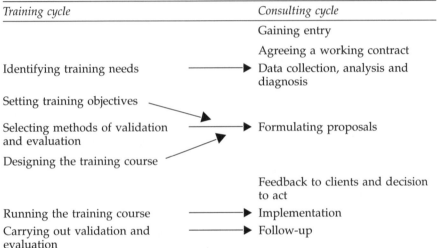

Training cycle	Consulting cycle
	Gaining entry
	Agreeing a working contract
Identifying training needs	Data collection, analysis and diagnosis
Setting training objectives	
Selecting methods of validation and evaluation	Formulating proposals
Designing the training course	
	Feedback to clients and decision to act
Running the training course	Implementation
Carrying out validation and evaluation	Follow-up

Juxtaposing the two cycles in this way gives us a rationale for the remainder of this chapter. First, we shall look briefly at the competences which a trainer familiar with all aspects of the training cycle can bring to consulting work. Secondly, we shall examine aspects of the consulting cycle for which trainers may be less well prepared. These centre on the need for continuous collaboration with clients throughout an assignment.

Competences gained from experience of the training cycle

The methods typically used to carry out a training needs survey provide many opportunities for developing useful tools and skills for the data collection stage of consulting. Trainers may examine job descriptions and person specifications or analyse the outcomes of appraisal systems. They may conduct a series of interviews with managers and their staff, design and administer questionnaires or use critical incident analysis.

Transferable competences:
- Contacts across functions and throughout the hierarchy.
- Knowledge of the organization.
- Interviewing skills.
- Observation skills.
- Analytical skills.
- Diagnostic skills (in terms of identifying training needs).

The next three stages of the training cycle involve the preparation of training programmes, from setting training objectives and designing a course, to the writing or selection of course materials. In effect the trainer produces a 'proposal' for meeting the training needs identified.

Transferable competences:
- Knowledge of various rationales, models and methodologies which underpin training design and training evaluation.
- Creative design skills.

The next stage involves organizing and running a series of training courses. This is the implementation stage.

Transferable competences:
- Planning and organizing skills in allocating staff resources, collating materials, arranging venues, managing budgets etc.
- Presentation skills.
- A wide range of interpersonal and process skills needed to run a training course.
- Understanding of and ability to manage group dynamics.

Some courses may involve pre-course briefing and post-course follow-up with participants, while those that involve more intensive personal learning may require the trainer to offer extra one-to-one support during the course.

Transferable competences:
- Feedback skills.
- Coaching skills.
- Counselling skills.

Finally, if methods of validation and evaluation involve more than end-of-course feedback sheets, then trainers will have the opportunity to assess the impact of the training in the work situation. This will mean returning to some of the activities carried out in stage 1 of the cycle.

A word of warning here. In our experience there are many trainers for whom the training cycle is more a theoretical concept than a true description of their work. This is borne out by the survey to which we have already referred in Chapter 2,[2] which showed that 'direct training' (i.e. stage 5, running training courses) was the main element of trainers' work. It is thus perfectly possible for trainers not to have developed the full range of competences listed here. Trainers who have gained experience in *all* the stages of the training cycle are better prepared for undertaking consulting work.

The nature of this development path

Looking again at the comparison between the two cycles, we see three stages in the consulting cycle which do not have parallels in the training cycle. These are the first two stages (gaining entry and agreeing working contracts) and stage 5 (feedback to clients and decision to act). We explain the differences in the following way.

As functional specialists, trainers do not need to gain entry to client managers, or to negotiate working contracts with them. It is their functional responsibility to identify and meet training needs in the organization and it is perfectly legitimate for the training department to make a unilateral decision to embark on a training needs survey. In other words, they can step straight into the data collection stage and are quite likely to take responsibility for deciding what data to collect, how to collect it and what to do with it. It is then perfectly possible for trainers to carry out the next three stages of the training cycle under the auspices of the training department, drawing solely on their own expertise.

The result of their efforts is likely to be the publication of a brochure of training courses, complete with dates, objectives, outline content and guidelines for eligibility for each course. Implementation of the courses then goes ahead as participants are nominated. Implicitly managers 'agree' to the proposals for the courses by attending them, but the decision to go ahead and run the programmes has been made by the training department.

Trainers do think of line managers *in general* as their clients, but as they become internal consultants, they need to negotiate working relationships with individual managers who will be the sponsoring clients for each consulting project. Trainers' experience of the training cycle may lead them to have a limited and limiting view of their role in this relationship; they may be more likely to adopt an expert position. This has been described as the 'physician's approach', i.e. the client presents symptoms and the consultant conducts an examination, makes a diagnosis and prescribes a remedy. The client remains relatively passive and dependent until the point at which he or she decides whether to implement the recommendations. At this point the position is reversed as the consultant waits to see if the client metaphorically tears up the prescription, pretends to accept it but never takes the pills, completes only part of the prescribed treatment or takes the medicine and, depending on the results, views the 'doctor' as a saviour or a quack.

It is now widely recognized that expert consulting is effective mainly for short-term problem-solving: it is characteristic of consulting in technical fields such as marketing, finance, computer technology and so on. It does not produce a lasting, self-sustaining change for the client. For this reason when we talk about consulting in this book, we shall be advocating a collaborative approach. This is because we are writing about consultancy whose prime purpose is client learning, whatever technical aspects to the assignment there may be.

To collaborate means to work together to create a partnership based on mutual trust and mutual recognition of each other's different contributions. Such an approach is characterized by three factors:

1　A relationship between consultant and client which is based on personal equality, regardless of differences in specialized knowledge, skill, age or hierarchical position.
2　A strong, jointly agreed working contract which is open to renegotiation by both parties.
3　Client involvement in all stages of the project.

In the remainder of this chapter we discuss these three characteristics in some detail, giving guidelines for trainers wanting to work as collaborative consultants.

Creating equal partnerships with clients

In Chapter 3 we discussed the nature of trainer–trainee relationships in the training room. The situation unfortunately arouses memories of school and echoes of teacher–pupil relationships. If trainers consciously or unconsciously reinforce this memory, then they may well invoke in course members a range of compliant, rebellious, passive or competitive behaviours in response. Some trainers will have learnt to recognize and accept the underlying dynamics of their relationships with training groups and will take great satisfaction in encouraging collaborative relationships as the course progresses. Some may do this implicitly, others, because of the objectives of the course, may do so more explicitly. Some of the issues, and certainly the skills needed to handle them, are just as valid when we look at the possible dynamics of consultant–client relationships.

For the internal consultant the seeds of personal inequality may lie in:

- A difference in hierarchical status between consultant and client manager.
- A previous relationship on a different basis such as trainer–course member or boss–subordinate.
- An organizational culture which includes line–specialist friction.

Both internal and external consultants may also have to contend with other issues in building relationships with their clients, such as:

- Clients' fixed preconceptions about trainers or consultants.
- Consultants' fixed preconceptions about managers.
- Consultants feeling under pressure to prove themselves.
- Clients wanting to abdicate responsibility to a consultant.
- Consultants over-eager to land an assignment.
- Clients who want to use consultants as temporary extra resources at their disposal.
- Unwilling clients being pressurized into using a consultant by their boss.
- Consultants' unexpressed anxieties about making a good impression, about being a possible scapegoat, about making a success of a project, about being helpful.
- Clients' unexpressed anxieties about being conned, about losing face, about staying in control, about avoiding 'sensitive' areas.

Many trainers will recognize these as process issues in the 'task, procedure and process' model of human interaction represented in Figure 4.1.

The *task* is the work that people set out to complete together, e.g. consultant and client meet to establish the goals of a consulting project. This is their task in this instance.

The *procedures* are the methods people choose for organizing themselves in achieving the task. For example, $1^1/_2$ hours are

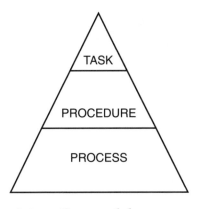

Figure 4.1   Human interaction model

allocated for a meeting. The client starts by outlining his or her thoughts. After some questioning and discussion with the consultant five points are logged on a whiteboard. The client agrees to expand these points in writing and send a copy to the consultant. The consultant agrees to write a proposal for the way in which the consulting assignment could progress, for discussion with the client at their next meeting. The consultancy cycle is a procedural model.

The *process* is the underlying feelings and motivations people bring to the task and to each other, e.g. whether consultant and/or client is scared, excited, defensive, suspicious, impatient, etc.; whether either feels that his or her neck is on the line. Whether each believes the other is being honest. Process is present at every stage of the consulting cycle. Some examples are given in Table 4.2.

As Figure 4.1 shows, *task* is the most accessible and obvious level in the interaction, the tip of the iceberg. It is the ostensible reason for the interaction. The *procedure* may be explicitly agreed or may emerge, partly in response to the demands of the task and partly as the way the process level is revealed. The *process* level is the least accessible, but is the foundation on which the task is built. As such, it governs the strength or weakness of the other layers and gives colour, life and character to the task and procedure. The origin of resistance is process,

Table 4.2   Process in consultancy

Stages	Consultant	Client
Gaining entry, establishing a working contract	• Will they like me? • Do they really need me? • Can I *really* help? • What are their real needs? • Do I want to do it? • Am I flavour of the month? • Do I like what I'm hearing/feeling? • Who really has the power/money? • Is this worth it?	• Can I trust this person? • Will I look a fool? • Are they trying to kid me? • Will I know if they are? • Am I comfortable with them? • Glad to have someone to talk to • Here comes a straw to clutch • Relief at sharing • Will they fit?
Gathering data, data analysis and diagnosis	• Self-doubt • How do I remember it all? • Reassessing type/ amount of involvement • Are they being honest with me? • Am I going down well? • Feeling pressure to deliver solutions • Am I asking the right questions?	• Why does he/she want to know that? • Worried about giving too much information • Get on with your job • Suspicion about methods • Relief at being understood • Am I alone in my view? • Will they come up with the information I want to hear? • This data can help me elsewhere • Will I have to account for answers?
Feedback and decision to act	• Can I really do this? • Am I right? • How do I package this? • What will this do for my reputation/ future employment? • How much commitment do they have?	• Does it fit in with the culture? • How much work for me? • Did I get my money's worth? • Already tried it • Fear, apprehension • How does this make me look?

Table 4.2 Continued		
	• Will this upset someone?	• Have I made the right choice?
	• Will they listen?	• What's in it for me?
	• What thing or things will persuade them?	• What am I getting myself into?
	• Will this get to the right people?	• Good, they see it my way!
	• Do they still like me?	
Implementation and monitoring	• Whose responsibility is it?	• Where's the support?
	• How's it going?	• Relief at last, someone is doing something
	• Are these the *real* issues?	• Comparisons with other consultants
	• How do they feel about me now?	• How can I criticize if I am not happy?
	• How do I withdraw?	• How can I give feedback?
	• Where's the support I was promised?	• It is a challenge
	• I wish they would stop checking on me	• What are they doing?
	• How can I ensure this is really used?	• How is the organization reacting?
Follow-up	• Will they hire me again?	• Gratitude
	• Do I want them to hire me?	• Fear of being on own
	• Did I get anywhere?	• Relief, something done
	• What have I learned?	• Do I want any further contact?
	• How can I help a client learn from experience?	• If so how do I go about it?
	• How can I help them in future relationships?	• Justify expenditure against payoff/ results?
	• Regrets at letting go	• When will I see results?
		• Could we have done it without them?
		• Thinking about bringing in someone else

even though it may well manifest itself through task or procedure. For example, a client may be fearful of what a series of diagnostic interviews may produce. However, rather than express these fears directly, she may dispute the types of questions being proposed for the interviews. This is by no means saying that resistance is by definition a 'bad thing'. It may simply be a sign that people believe they are moving beyond their capacity to cope. It is important, therefore, to deal with process, either directly or indirectly, right from the outset of meetings with clients. It is easier to build an equal relationship to begin with than break the mould of an unequal one later on.

The following are the key components in the process of establishing equal relationships with clients:

1   Having a strong base of self-esteem.
2   Listening to clients.
3   Refusing to be rushed through the contracting stage.
4   Expressing the consultant's wants for the project as well as finding out what the client wants.
5   Paying attention to any feelings of unease experienced during early meetings.
6   Being willing to ask direct questions.
7   Giving and eliciting feedback on the progress of the relationship.

Let us look more closely at each in turn.

Self-esteem

For trainers moving into consultancy, leaving behind the security of a familiar role, self-confidence may be at a low ebb. Before meeting a potential client it may help trainers to remember the wide range of skill and experience they already have – the transferable competences outlined earlier in this chapter. Furthermore, they should be able to recognize the type of client remarks that deflate their self-confidence and consider possible responses. The best response is to maintain an attitude of curiosity rather than become defensive, e.g.:

Client: We've tried something like that before and it was a disaster.
Consultant: What happened? What do we need to pay attention to this time, in order to avoid similar problems?

Client: How much do you really understand about the pressures we're under here?

Consultant: What else do you think it's important that I understand?

Although consultants offer specialist knowledge and skills, they do not need to put themselves under pressure to come up with instant answers to everything. On the contrary, a consultant who wants to appear to know all the answers risks encouraging a relationship in which the client accepts or rejects the consultant's proposals but has no ownership in them.

Listening to the client

Often new consultants believe they will need to impress potential clients by selling themselves and their services. However, what clients most want is understanding of their concerns, needs and priorities from someone who is realistic and confident about how he or she can help. The main skills in early meetings therefore are good listening, asking good questions and the capacity to express understanding of the client's view of the project, including its special features and the client's desired outcomes. Very often consultants establish credibility with clients at this stage not by offering anything new but simply by reflecting back accurately what has been said to them. True collaboration in consultancy means working together on the *client's* concerns, not the consultant's favourite intervention. For trainers this may mean not using jargon to sound clever and not distorting what the client is saying to fit a training intervention they know how to run.

Contracting well

Clients who pride themselves on being action managers in a culture that rewards this will put themselves and others under pressure to get on and do something fast. Resist this temptation until a solid working contract has been agreed. At this point the consultants' knowledge of what needs to be covered in each phase of the consulting cycle may be the particular contribution they bring to the collaboration. Being assertive about this is one way of establishing personal equality in the early meetings. Consultants who find themselves talking about the design for an intervention at the start of the first meeting with a client are clearly being seduced or bullied into premature action, or else are themselves uncomfortable about resolving the process issues of the contracting stage. We shall say more about this later in the chapter.

Negotiating wants and offers

It is a common error for consultants to concentrate exclusively on finding out what their clients want from them. Although obviously important, this can lead to a one-sided, unequal relationship. At one extreme the consultant becomes a Uriah Heep character, obsequiously striving to satisfy the client's wishes. At the other extreme the consultant can be in danger of becoming a super-hero, promising too much and allowing unrealistic expectations. Balance is achieved by the consultant's willingness to talk about such things as:

- What I can and cannot do.
- What my own values are.
- What I will *need* from you, the client, to ensure success in the project.
- What I *want* from you, the client, in order to work at my best.
- What I want from the project to meet my own need for satisfaction and achievement.

Expressing views in these areas gives the opportunity for consultant and client to negotiate as equals about what they want from, and what they can offer to, the project and each other. Obviously in order to do this, consultants need to have thought carefully about what collaboration means to them and what it is appropriate for them to ask for, e.g.:

- 'Before I begin I would like you to brief the staff I shall be interviewing about the background to this project.'

- 'I would like you to include me in that meeting you are arranging with X.'
- 'I want us to agree some form of joint evaluation of this project about six months after its completion.'
- 'I think your involvement in the team-building will be very important. How much time are you willing to give to this?'

Noticing feelings of unease

Vague feelings of unease or discomfort are sure signs that important process issues are not being dealt with. It is tempting for consultants to ignore or dismiss them if they are over-anxious to get work, or keen to please their clients at all costs or reluctant to rock the boat; but we have learnt that it is never worth while. One must recognize the unease, pinpoint its cause and consciously choose when and how to raise the issue.

We were once invited by another consultant to consider the possibility of becoming part of a European consultant team which her client, a multinational company based in America, was assembling. Attracted by the apparent glamour of the assignment, we were keen to become involved and travelled to a location on the Continent to take part in a pilot programme.

The consultants our colleague had recommended were to participate in the programme and then be involved in design meetings for progressing the project in Europe. We were welcomed warmly and in the midst of the general bonhomie it was all too easy to submerge the vague doubts we had about the basis for our involvement, which had been 'sorted out' between the client and our American colleague. On the final day it emerged that the event was being used as a way of assessing the consultants. The anger, defensiveness and mistrust that was generated at that meeting severely strained relationships and was a setback for both consultants *and* clients.

On later reflection we knew that we had suspected the truth in our hearts but had colluded in not facing it. This is a fairly extreme example, but all twinges of unease, if denied instead of explored, weaken the ground on which really collaborative relationships can be built.

Asking direct questions

Following on from the last point, we have found that consultants can avoid colluding with their clients if they ask seemingly naïve or awkward questions. It is interesting to speculate on the extent to which clients really want to change things when they call in consultants. What has been learned about the nature of change is that it involves at least some degree of loss, pain and confusion before new direction is established. So it is perfectly possible that consultants and clients may seek each other out in order to create the appearance of change while actually avoiding it. The consultant's willingness to confront issues in a timely way is one signal of a healthy rather than collusive relationship. The skills involved may well have been acquired by trainers who use constructive challenge to help people learn by, for example:

- Asking questions that are simple and direct.
- Watching out for redefinition, i.e. a different question being answered than the one asked.
- Quietly persisting in asking the question again, immediately or later.
- Tolerating silence and giving the client time to respond rather than answering the question oneself or defending having asked it.

Awkward questions are often needed to explore the opposite of whatever is being comfortably talked about. For example:

- Doubts and risks when the client is only expressing confidence and optimism.
- Short-term implications when only long-term issues are being discussed.
- Other parties involved when the client is talking as if this is a personal pet project.
- What the client actually *wants* when the discussion has

concentrated on what ought to happen or what the situation demands.

In other words, this is where a consultant needs to stay out of the client's frame of reference as well as being able to step into it.

Exchanging feedback

Since the quality of the consultant–client relationship is such an important part of consulting, it is a good idea to be able to talk about it. Relationships can become productive most quickly if both sides are operating not with assumptions about each other's reactions but with real information about the effect they are having on one another. This is an area where trainers usually have skills, as long as they are accustomed to *exchanging* feedback rather than giving it most of the time or only asking for it formally at the end of a course. Consultants might want to find out what led the client to want to work with him or her in particular, to ask in what ways he or she is being helpful or unhelpful, and to review the effectiveness of the collaboration at regular intervals.

Crucially one is holding one's work up for scrutiny, but the timing and the manner are important. For example, at the end of the first meeting one consultant rather baldly asked, 'So what do you think of me?' The embarrassment was almost tangible and intimidated the client. Also, exchanging feedback does not mean being totally open about everything. The client is not paying to be burdened by all the consultant's insecurities, big or small. The consultant should be taking these to a supervisor, counsellor, colleague or support group.

Agreeing an effective working contract

This involves consultant and client agreeing what it is they aim to achieve together, how they are going to set out doing this and who is responsible for what. This agreement is not intended to force compliance between the parties, as in a legal contract. Its purpose is to clarify conditions that will give the project the greatest chance of success. Because the tasks of the contracting stage sound straightforward and obvious enough, it is easy to underestimate the care needed to contract well. Probably all consultants would agree that problems arising in later stages of an assignment can be traced back to poor initial contracting or failure to renegotiate the contract as circumstances change.

Training contracts

Trainers often do not spend a great deal of time explicitly contracting with trainees. A training course is published, with dates, aims and outline of contents and methods. In doing this trainers are stating their side of the contract. In arriving for the course trainees implicitly accept the contract but, as many trainers know to their cost, this very limited type of contracting gives no guarantee that there is real understanding between the parties about their expectations of one another.

Some trainers seek to overcome this by engaging in some further contracting at the start of a course. They may outline the course objectives again, and explain their role and their expectations of course members. Unfortunately they are likely to get very quick acceptance of whatever they propose. At this stage of a course trainees are all too willing to be dependent (and even insistent) on the trainer taking leadership.

Some trainers go further in encouraging an exchange of expectations about the course, devoting time to agreeing which ones they are and are not able or willing to meet, and seeking the same information from participants; but it is in many ways already too late for this dialogue. The course has started, and the area open to change by negotiation is inevitably limited. Even when trainers take care to provide extensive briefing notes for participants or arrange to speak with them before the course, this is less about contracting than about selection.

Compared with consulting relationships, the lack of solid contracting that characterizes so many training courses can be tolerated because:

1   The parameters of the relationship between trainer and trainee are relatively clear-cut and short term.

2 The task they are working on together does not involve live organizational issues, so that less is at stake.

None the less lack of clarity and mutual understanding about aims and responsibilities does lead to all sorts of problems on courses:

- 'Difficult' course members.
- Rejection of the trainer and/or the course material.
- Dissatisfaction for trainer and trainees.
- Wasted time and resources.

Trainers who have experienced these problems, no matter how well planned their courses, need to appreciate that strong contracts in consulting are even more important.

Consulting contracts[3]
It may take one or several meetings to arrive at a consulting contract. Some relationships will never progress to this stage. Some perfectly legitimate outcomes from the first meeting with a client could be:

- Consultant and client agree *not* to embark on a project together and both understand why not.
- Initial contact is made and the door is open for further visits but the client is still a potential rather than an actual client.
- Consultant agrees to write a proposal for working with the client (draft contract) to be discussed at a further meeting.
- Consultant and client agree the basis of a contract. Perhaps dates are to be decided. A phone call or letter is needed to confirm the contract.
- All aspects of a working contract are agreed at the meeting.

Although a written contract is not necessary, it is very helpful in testing mutual understanding. (Is what *you* think I said the same as what *I* think I said and did we mean the same by these words anyway?)

There is no single way of writing a contract – it may be

informal or formal, a lengthy document, a letter or just a set of points. Subsequent chapters give some examples. The elements that need to be covered are:

1   Brief summary of the background and need for the project (the context).
2   The aims and objectives of the project.
3   Who is involved and who is responsible for doing what.
4   The agreed first steps.
5   Timescales and fees.

There are two areas we would like to discuss further. One is the difficulty of defining who is actually the client and the second is the often awkward subject of consultant time and how to charge for it.

Who is the client?

Trainers have no problem defining who their trainees are. Everyone who has enrolled on a course is a course member and the primary contract is between trainer and trainees for the duration of the course. Sometimes there are complications when trainers are expected to report back in some way to nominating managers or other interested parties, but in our experience most trainers resist being placed in this position, arguing that it does not produce a helpful learning climate. It is also true that trainers are under contract to their own managers in the training department but this type of contract is the same as that between all employees and their managers and is supervisory in nature, unlike contracts negotiated where there are no direct hierarchical relationships.

Consultants need to contract in some way with a number of different people on any particular assignment. They are interested in finding out:

• Who is the person with the real authority to commission the consultant's services? This person as the sponsor has the ultimate say in which and how many resources are available for the project. He or she may or may not be the first person that the consultant meets regarding the project.

- Who is the main person with whom the consultant will collaborate (the liaison)? If this is not the same person as the sponsor, a clear three-way contract will be needed.
- Are the sponsor and/or the liaison beneficiaries of the project, i.e. are they committed to its outcomes or is there a less visible beneficiary exerting pressure somewhere?
- Is there a target group on whom the project is intended to impact? The contract with the sponsor needs to be clear about how this group will become involved in the project.
- Are there other parties who will be affected in some way by the project? To what extent, when and how do they need to be involved?

The consultant's job is to reconnoitre this territory, establish who is who and have clear agreements about how he or she is going to work with the different members of the client system. Such a job may be easier for the internal consultant who is familiar with the formal and informal structure of the organization than the external consultant, who needs to gather this information in the early stages by asking direct questions and not taking anything for granted.

Another aspect of reconnoitring the territory is finding out whether other consultants are or have been involved with the client system. One colleague told us how he undertook extensive work on a project only to be told his proposals nearly duplicated those of an earlier consultant. If he had found out that a previous consulting intervention had been made, he could have saved a lot of time and, probably more importantly, realized that the real problem was a reluctance in the client system to take productive action. They preferred to keep researching the problem than actually to implement change.

Estimating consultant time

This aspect of contracting can be an awkward one for both consultants and clients. It is one that external consultants cannot avoid; nor can those growing numbers of internal consultants who, operating from a profit-centre, are charging for their services. We would argue that even if this is not the case, internal consultants need to place a value on their own time in order to contract professionally and to have a basis for assessing different assignments, choosing between them and organizing their workload. Internal consultants who do not contract for their time can easily over-commit themselves, allow unrealistic timescales or undertake projects that are not viable in business terms.

The points we make below about fees are therefore also relevant for talking about consultant time as a finite and valuable resource, whether or not pound signs are attached. In fact consultant time is not what the client is really buying, rather it is the quality of the consultant's concentrated attention during that time.

Deciding on fee levels

It is important for consultants to have a basis for charging fees that takes into account market rates, their own level of experience and the sort of consultancy services they offer. For trainers there may need to be a mental switch in charging for themselves and their time rather than charging for a course or places on a course. This is a vital distinction. For example, someone selling training packages may quote an all-in fee for running a course for a fixed number of participants, with associated meetings and other preparation included – a sales rather than a consulting approach. What a consultant should assess is the amount of time needed to undertake all or part of a proposed project, and multiply it by a daily fee. Deciding on a daily rate enables consultants to be clear and assertive in stating their fees at the outset of a contract with a potential client. The cost of the project is then allied to what the client wants to achieve and how much time the consultant estimates it will take. If the cost is too much, the client can consider:

- Using a consultant with a lower fee rate.
- Questioning the consultant's estimate of time needed for different aspects of the project.

- Reviewing the scope of the project and setting more limited objectives.
- Agreeing to a pilot or first stage, after which further work can be agreed.

Dealing with fees in this way enables both parties to handle more comfortably the underlying anxieties that talking about time and money can arouse. For example, these could be:

Client	*Consultant*
Am I being taken advantage of?	Am I being taken advantage of?
How do I know what I'm buying?	Am I selling myself short?
Should I haggle?	Will I be seen as over-rating myself?

Fixed rate

Trainers who see running courses as their main work can be tempted to charge a lower rate for other sorts of activity. Charging less for data collection, interviews, design and follow-up work encourages all parties to devalue these aspects of the consultant's contribution. They are seen as adjuncts to a training course and promote the image of a trainer rather than a consultant. In fact a lot more than image is at stake if the consultant does not give due weight to the pre-implementation stages of consultancy, for symptoms are distinguished from causes during these stages, underlying problems are identified, tailored interventions are designed and client involvement and commitment are cemented. These are the areas where the consultant's contribution is most valuable and should be charged for. The shift of emphasis probably comprises the single most important change of attitude that helps trainers make the transition to consultancy.

Reduced fees

There may be occasions when consultants agree to a reduced fee because they particularly want to be involved in a project as a result of personal conviction or seeing it as offering them a unique development opportunity. In order to maintain the effectiveness of contracting it is important that such an agreement is made openly and honestly.

Consultants who allow themselves to be jockeyed into accepting a reduced fee can easily resent this later and consciously or unconsciously give less than their best. Even if this does not happen, they may be overloading themselves, making up the lost fees by taking on extra work elsewhere, and thereby reducing their effectiveness.

In addition, offering a low fee as a way of getting work in the early days can be a trap that corners a consultant into being seen as cut-rate. It is difficult to increase rates after gaining entry without the risk of the client feeling cornered; and it is futile secretly to underestimate the time needed for a project, when a vicious circle is thus created in which future realistic estimates are seen as inflated. The important thing is for consultants to be honest with their clients and themselves.

Encouraging client involvement

A collaborative approach involves an attitude of mind and some explicitly negotiated agreements. Once this is achieved, consultants and clients can find many possibilities for joint work throughout a consulting contract. We outline below some of the possibilities, and Chapters 5, 7 and 9 contain examples of collaborative consultancy in practice:

- Decide together what information is needed, who has it and how to collect it; involve the client's resources in the actual collection.
- Summarize and present data to the client in a descriptive way, for joint analysis and diagnosis; invite those who supplied the data to extract the significance; offer interpretations and observations as suggestions only; focus on avoided areas and encourage debate.
- Engage in joint design work. Provide frameworks and ideas

and invite the client's comments and additions; outline options and help clients choose; aim to achieve joint ownership of proposals; present ideas together to senior management or act as third parties in discussions between interested groups.

- During implementation, neither leave clients completely unsupported nor 'do it for them'; if running a development event is involved, ask clients to attend, or co-work with them on different aspects of the programme.
- Review progress together regularly.
- At the end of the project, discuss lessons learnt and future directions for both parties.

A collaborative relationship once established cannot then be taken for granted, but requires regular attention. One can easily become immersed in the detail of the tasks and lose sight of the process. Some possible indications that all is not well include:

- Clients becoming repeatedly 'unavailable'.
- Insufficient time being allocated for meetings.
- Consultants being steered towards client contacts without the authority to make decisions.
- Clients wanting more and more detail.
- The consultant's credentials being questioned.
- Clients suddenly becoming compliant, agreeing with everything the consultant says.

Signals such as these indicate that mutual trust is faltering. It takes courage not to accept them at face value, but to find opportunities to state in a clear, non-threatening and non-defensive way what the consultant is experiencing, so that concerns can be openly discussed and resolved rather than avoided.

In this chapter we have described the nature of the development path for those moving from training to consulting. The challenge for many trainers is acquiring skills in building and maintaining collaborative relationships with clients. The next chapter provides one example of what this can mean in practice.

Notes

1   Block, P. *Flawless Consulting: A Guide to Getting Your Expertise Used*, Learning Concepts 1981.
2   Bennett, R. (ed) *Improving Trainer Effectiveness*, Gower 1988.
3   Freedman, A.M. 'Client/Consultant Contact Problems', in Lee, R.J. and Freedman, A.M. (eds) *Consultation Skills Reading*, NTL Institute 1984.

5 The training consultant

This chapter has three sections. First, we consider ways of 'gaining entry', since this is often a worry for those just starting to move into consultancy. Although the phrase 'gaining entry' is commonly used, it has a belligerent ring to it. One can infer that there is a stronghold to be breached, resistance to be broken. This perspective is not an auspicious start for a productive relationship. With this major caveat we describe some of the ways consultants can create opportunities to do their work. Secondly, there is a description of a consulting assignment carried out by an internal consultant. Thirdly, we compare internal and external consultant roles and outline their probable strengths and weaknesses.

Creating opportunities

Training consultants with established reputations can expect potential clients to seek their services at least some of the time. In the transition period trainers are often more concerned with gaining access to managers through their own initiative. Here are some ideas for gaining entry, starting with approaches which are most readily available to trainers and progressing to those which become more appropriate as experience increases:

1   Follow-up meetings with selected course members.
2   Widening the scope of a training needs survey.
3   Special projects requiring research with managers.
4   Mounting a special event to spark interest in consultancy.
5   Self-education visits.
6   Using insider knowledge to target potential clients.
7   Joint publishing (with clients) in in-house journals.

Post-course follow-up

The debriefing of participants after a course is often the responsibility of the nominating manager unless some form of follow-up and evaluation has been planned as part of the training. Many trainers are prevented from doing as much follow-up with course members as they would like, because of the demands that regular direct training makes on their time.

The post-course meeting is an obvious consultancy opportunity and for this purpose it is easier to be selective about which people to arrange to see. For example:

- Those participants with whom the trainer has already established a relationship of mutual respect and who are clearly keen to apply and develop further the course material.
- Those participants in a position to sponsor the development of others and who have the power to make decisions.
- Those from a team or department who are nominating significant numbers for a training programme. Perhaps a tailored version would be a more efficient and effective use of resources.
- Those from a part of the organization notable for *not* nominating many people for training courses (a rare chance to gain entry perhaps).

It is a relatively simple matter for trainers to start viewing course members as potential clients and to arrange follow-up meetings during a programme. A three-way meeting to include the participant's boss is a useful way of gaining entry to a higher level in the organization. A review of the application of course learning gives the trainer the opportunity to open the discussion to wider issues in the manager's area of responsibility.

Widening the scope of a training needs survey

Trainers usually design data collection to uncover generalized training needs; they may thereby also acquire useful information on where there may be opportunities for consultancy. We also know several training departments that launched themselves into consulting work by giving managers the opportunity to request it. Rather than asking about training needs, they conducted surveys that invited managers to describe what services they needed to manage development in the organization. As we noted in Chapter 2, many managers' requirements can be better met by internal consultancy than standard training courses, and responses to the survey reflected this. This strategy implies that the training department is willing to encourage possible criticism and complaint from its customers, in order to fuel and support change.

Taking on special projects

Any project that gives a trainer a legitimate reason for arranging meetings with key managers throughout the organization is an opportunity to gain entry. We spoke to several trainers whose internal consultancy careers began in this way. One researched proposals for setting up the training and development function as a business centre, another undertook the revision of forms used for appraisal purposes and another looked at the successes and difficulties faced by groups of participants on training courses who resolved to continue meeting after courses in order to promote mutual development. All became adept at widening the discussion from their initial entry point in order to uncover possible consulting opportunities.

Mounting a special event

Organizing one-off 'management briefings' on a topic of current organizational concern was the method one group of trainers used to initiate dialogue with managers and stimulate interest in further collaboration. Themes included:

- 'Stress at work – how do we identify and manage it?'
- 'Do we need more entrepreneurs?'
- 'Vision-building: how is it different from strategic planning?'
- 'Corporate culture: let's look at ours.'

The trainers' aim was to introduce potential clients to new ideas in ways that invited joint exploration of their usefulness and relevance for current management concerns. This approach lends itself to a fruitful collaboration between internal and external consultants. The external provides a focus, bringing in particular knowledge and experience. Externals are sometimes given a hearing where internal people are not, and they have the opportunity to ask important, naïve or difficult questions. The internal consultant can provide an in-company point of view on the material, brief the external consultant on what issues to focus on and build interest and contacts. The collaboration is usually more productive than either party working independently.

The more such events can become a forum for discussion rather than just presentation, the greater the opportunity for contact with managers on the basis of joint problem identification. A variety of formats, such as working lunches, breakfasts, or an after-hours colloquium, as well as a half- or one-day seminar, all offer the chance of gaining entry and building consultant–client rather than trainer–trainee relationships. The 'swap-shop' meetings held by the Association for Management Education and Development (see p. 207 for its address) are organized along these lines.

Doing this well means keeping up to date with current issues in the organization and linking these with professional knowledge and contacts in a wider field. This sort of homework is essential anyway for building competence and credibility as a consultant.

Self-education visits

The need to keep informed of organizational issues and trends is a continuing necessity in consulting. Peters and Austin[1] have popularized the strategy of MBWA (Managing by Walking About). The similar strategy of LBWA (Learning by Walking About) is one that consultants can use for the dual purpose of self-education and gaining entry. We have found that as long as consultants do not pick the week before the budget has to be submitted or another equally fraught time, then managers are very willing to talk about their own experience, ideas and concerns. A visit on this basis is more welcome than a sales call as long as it is genuine. Managers can become understandably resentful when an educational visit suddenly turns into a hard sell. Listening attentively, asking good questions, demonstrating understanding and offering some fresh thoughts and ideas in exchange, are forms of behaviour more likely to impress a potential client than any amount of persuasive sales talk.

Although this approach sows seeds for the future rather than producing immediate results, a proportion of such visits are likely to lead eventually to consulting assignments. For the less experienced consultant, this is also an opportunity to practise consulting skills with minimal risk. The starting point can be anything from the straightforward 'I would like to understand more about the work of your department and the particular challenges facing you as its manager', to something more specific, such as 'I'm interested in your views about the impact new technology has made in your department' or 'I'm writing an article on the Manager as Developer and I would like to discuss some of the points with you'.

Using insider knowledge

One internal consultant said he used his knowledge of the company to identify 'pain points' in the organization where managers were under pressure owing to planned reorganization, high turnover, expansion, the introduction of new systems, or poor morale. He would approach those he saw to be 'in pain' and ready for change with an offer to explore with them ways in which he could offer consulting help. He gained his information through an informal network of contacts and by scanning records and plans. He gained entry by making an appearance in times of difficulty and acquiring a reputation as a valuable resource to a trouble-shooting team. Another consultant we spoke to said her tactic was to identify people moving into new positions in the organization. She would time a visit at the point when they might be most open to changing things and interested in initiating new ventures.

Publishing

Once consulting projects are in progress, it is possible to publicize them by writing up the work in an in-house journal. Co-authoring with a client manager, describing honestly both the successes and the learning from whatever difficulties arose, is a way of ensuring that the piece excites the interests of other managers. Here the consultant is writing for potential clients rather than professional colleagues. A variant of this is producing 'how to' guides (e.g. interviewing, training needs analysis). If they are genuinely useful they can enhance the visibility and standing of the training consultant.

Points for external consultants

Most of what we have written above applies to the internal consultant. Consultants who are not selling packaged approaches which can be marketed tend to rely on building a reputation that will encourage new clients to contact them. Most use some or all of the following:

- Attending/presenting at national and international professional conferences.
- Publishing in journals/writing books.
- Mounting a few open programmes to give people a 'taste' of their work.
- Forming peer networks, where colleagues offer each other entry opportunities.

- Becoming associates of institutes or university departments which offer consultancy services.
- Becoming members of professional bodies that act as referral agencies for consultants or furnish potential clients with lists of accredited members.

A training consultancy assignment

As a way of illustrating in more detail the work of the training consultant there follow some extracts from a report written by an internal consultant, whom we shall call Alison Wright. We met as a result of carrying out a team-building and consultancy skills programme for the training group to which she belonged. Originally she had written some notes solely for her own use but then agreed to expand them for inclusion in this book. Her organization was a large insurance company and her department (Training and Development) had recently become a profit-centre. Names have been changed to preserve confidentiality.

Background to the assignment
I had run quite a number of assertiveness programmes for my company but these had all been on an 'open' basis. When David Franklin, the personnel manager, rang me to discuss a special course for the new graduate intake, I was pleased, but a little nervous. I was not used to negotiating about costs and I did not know David that well, although I had met some of his staff on courses.

The first interview
I went to David's office and he quickly said that he had heard good things about me and my courses. He had seen the programme description and objectives for an assertiveness skills course and he was sure it was just right for the particular group he had in mind. The reason for the training, he said, was that the graduates (average age 25) were technically highly competent, but many of them failed to make contributions at meetings, allowed themselves to be talked down, and generally

seemed slow to take initiatives. They were all coming to the end of their year-long probationary period, known as the Graduate Development Programme, and it was intended that the course would help them to be successful in moving on to a permanent appointment.

In response I had a strong inclination simply to say yes, particularly since Training and Development (T & D) had been wanting to build bridges with the personnel department for some time and I wanted to be seen as helpful. However, just as I was reminding myself not to take everything at face value, David made the additional comment that he would want reports on each of the participants. Their performance on the course would form part of the final assessment of the probationary period. I replied that reports were not normally made on course participants and that I believed it was only through a strict rule of confidentiality that people would be sufficiently open about themselves and each other to be able to acquire assertiveness skills.

After some further probing I discovered that his real concern was with one individual, Paul, a borderline case who might fail the probationary period because of his quietness. Eventually David agreed that it did not make sense to jeopardize the programme and that an informal follow-up with Paul would be the best way of approaching the problem. So, in addition to the follow-up work which I would undertake, David would see each person individually.

The discussion about Paul led me to be rather more cautious and I decided that it really would be important for me to do some preliminary work, meet each of the intended participants and find out more about their training needs. There was another reason for this. One of my colleagues was having difficulty in another part of the organization because not enough attention had been paid to preliminary work. A group of managers had been brought together to attend a course on managing change. They were responsible for various local offices where a lot of new technology was being introduced. The course had been halted after half a day because the group were furious about the lack of support they were getting, in particular delays in the installation of new equipment. I did not want to find myself in such a position because I had not investigated the context for the training.

David was surprised about my insistence on the need for preliminary work but I felt that I would rather risk losing the assignment than get into the same mess as my colleague. I held my ground, explaining my reasons, and we reached agreement on some preliminary interviews.

The working contract
I felt generally happy about how the discussions had gone. However, I did not feel that I had achieved a fully collaborative relationship. It was as if I was being employed, rather than we were jointly seeking to solve a problem. Having talked to one of my colleagues, I decided that I could perhaps change the relationship a little by getting David involved in decisions about the data collection. I included this in my letter to him:

Dear David,
I am writing to confirm our agreements of last Thursday when we discussed the running of an assertiveness programme for last year's graduate intake. The objectives for this programme would be that they:

- Acquire an increased sense of self-confidence.
- Become more willing to express their views to senior managers.
- Contribute more fully to the interdisciplinary project teams to which they belong.

The programme will be highly participative, based on real work problems, with plenty of opportunity for skill development.
We agreed that a total of 3 days' preliminary work would be necessary:

- One and a half days of interviews, to identify the participants' particular training needs.
- One and a half days to analyse the data and finalize the course design.

When I have gathered my thoughts for the interview I would like to check with you to see if you have any additions or comments. I would also like you to brief the graduates about the proposed programme before the interviews.

We agreed that the course would be residential, probably lasting 3 days, to be followed by a 1-day meeting with the group to review their progress.

I will maintain confidentiality about individuals, although I will let you know in general terms whether I felt the objectives were met.

The only unknown which concerns me at this stage is that the data collected from the participants may lead us to reconsider the focus or emphasis of the training. At this stage the estimate of my time for this project is 7 days at the fee rate we discussed, namely £— per day.

I shall ring you next week to check any queries or concerns you might have.

Yours sincerely,

ALISON WRIGHT

Data collection

A week later I had confirmation that I could go ahead to the next stage. At our next brief meeting I tried to raise with David the questions that should be put to the graduates during the interviews, but he was not interested and I decided to let the matter drop. He seemed to think I should know what to ask and he did not have much time to talk then. I decided that, when interviewing the graduates, I would give an explanation of why the course was being proposed, a rough outline of the content and then ask them:

- 'Do you think you have needs in this area?'
- 'Are there any particular problems you have encountered?'
- 'What do you think of the proposed course?'
- 'Do you have any suggestions about other areas which might usefully be covered?'

I also wanted to gather some additional information about how they were feeling about their training generally and any other factors which might influence their attitude to the course.

Having carried out the interviews, I found the important data which emerged were:

- Several were suspicious about the proposed training, believing it masked an adverse judgement which had not been communicated directly.
- Most of them agreed that they did want help in being more assertive (in some instances this was confirmed by how they actually behaved during the interview).
- There was widespread dissatisfaction about the Graduate Development Programme. They felt that either they were being thrown in at the deep end, with too much being expected of them too soon, or else they were put in 'non-jobs' where they were bored.
- Most of the group felt under considerable stress.
- Four members of the group shared a flat and spent a lot of social time together.

With these data in mind I had a number of concerns:

- Those that were living together might be unwilling to give each other honest feedback; or alternatively they might bring too many domestic issues to the course.
- Assertiveness might be too narrow a focus, bearing in mind the other needs they had expressed.
- The course might become a dumping ground for bad feelings about the organization. Like the managers on the change course, they might be so resentful that they would be unwilling to look at how they themselves might improve.

I was also beginning to have doubts about whether one trainer would be enough, and I was regretting not having mentioned at any stage the possibility that two trainers might be needed. Maybe I had let possessiveness about the project get in the way of good sense.

Some of these concerns I was able to resolve in my own mind.

Regarding the close personal relationships it seemed to me that this issue could be raised at the beginning of the course and that agreement could probably be reached between us on the best way to manage this. The course content also did not appear to be an insuperable obstacle; it would be relatively easy to redesign so that other organizational skills, e.g. stress management and time management, could be included as well as assertiveness.

However, the question of the graduates' resentment about their training in general was something I needed to discuss with David.

The proposal

I did not want to go into print with my concerns, even though David was expecting a written report. I knew that the matter of graduate recruitment was a source of some intense debate in the personnel department. I did not want any document that I might produce to be used for fighting a minor political battle, especially one where I was unsure about David's position.

I raised these points with him when we met. His first reaction was one of surprise at the degree of resentment; but then we both decided that since assertiveness was one of the training needs, it was perhaps not surprising that they had restricted expression of their feelings to moaning sessions with each other; perhaps anyway they were afraid that any expression of dissatisfaction would be held against them in the final assessment. It also revealed a lack of consistent monitoring and feedback to the graduates about their progress. David seized on this eagerly, as it clearly confirmed one of his own concerns about the way the Graduate Development Programme was operating.

We achieved common ground and indeed a more collaborative relationship when we both recognized that some genuine training needs should not be sacrificed for the sake of fuelling a political debate that was highly unlikely to be resolved for some time to come. We agreed that we should raise and deal with the graduates' feelings about their induction in a way that was integrated into the design of the course.

David was much less accommodating when I said that maybe

I would need an additional trainer to help me. He was loath to pay the extra money and felt that with my experience of running assertiveness courses I should have known what the proper resourcing was likely to be.

After some discussion we linked the two problems and came up with a single solution. David agreed that he would work with me for part of the course. In this way he would be able to get some direct feedback about the Graduate Development Programme; also the participants would have the chance to practise their assertiveness skills.

With this issue dealt with there was little disagreement over extending the length of the course to include a wider range of topics.

This meeting had turned out to be the most difficult part of the whole assignment, but I was now in a position to put forward a formal written proposal:

Dear David,

As agreed at our last meeting I enclose the objectives and outline design for the training programme.

The main change from our initial thinking is the inclusion of a session when you will visit the group to discuss the Graduate Development Programme. I think that this may provide some useful information on which you can build, and the participants themselves will be able to practise their assertion skills; I shall do my best to discourage a 'dumping session', although I think that inevitably it will be partly such. My suggestion is that you send each person a briefing letter about the programme, explaining the purpose of your session so they can gather their thoughts. I shall ring you soon to discuss this further.

A follow-up day will take place about a month after the course, when progress on the action plans will be reviewed. Our hope is that you will be able to attend that day, but we agreed to make a final decision nearer the time.

I should also like to confirm that another 2 days of my time is required because of the course being lengthened and some additional design work being required.

I feel that we have found a good way of handling some potentially difficult areas and believe that the course stands every chance of being successful.

Yours sincerely,

ALISON WRIGHT

Implementation and follow-up

The course went well, although the session when David came down was difficult for me to handle. In particular I sometimes needed to be an intermediary, focusing everybody on the quality of their communication and ensuring that key points were logged. The review of the session from the perspective of people's assertion skills was very helpful.

The follow-up in this assignment consisted of more than the follow-up day itself. I arranged a meeting with David some three months after the course. In considering the project as a whole, we were pleased with the outcomes and that we had been able to insulate the training from the organizational politics. David expressed appreciation that I had insisted on the preliminary work, although he had had doubts about it at the time. There was no immediate possibility of further work together, so we both saw this as a suitable point for closure.

Commentary

In reviewing the project with us, Alison was generally pleased. She felt that she had been successful in a number of ways:

- Probing beyond the client's initial statements, e.g. uncovering the real reason why David wanted reports on the participants.
- Undertaking some preliminary data collection rather than offering an immediate packaged solution to the client's first perception of the problem. We pointed out to her that she had still found it difficult to let go of course design until *after* she had investigated the target group's training needs.

Her interviews were centred on an outline programme she had already prepared, thus guiding everyone's thinking in the same direction. She agreed that she had found it difficult to approach the interviews with an open, curious mind and had taken the course design with her as a prop.

- Building a collaborative relationship with her client. Alison felt that she had achieved this by continually discussing and resolving with David the issues raised by the programme. By engaging in joint problem-solving, her sense of being 'under instructions' had dissolved. She recognized that each time she had faced and talked through a potentially difficult area it had taken some courage on her part but had always proved rewarding. She agreed that it was important to aim for collaboration when it really mattered rather than use it as a technique. For example, trying to involve David in formulating interview questions, in this case, was inappropriate, in contrast to her proposal that he should work with her on the course when the graduates were invited to air their views of the induction programme.
- Checking agreements made. Alison said that writing to David about her understanding of their discussions had been an important discipline and had helped her to shape the progress of the assignment.
- Renegotiating her contract. Alison realized that initially she had been overly keen to prove herself and to be able to claim sole credit for any success in handling the assignment. She felt that she needed to be more willing to ask for help from her colleagues. She would then have considered earlier the possibility of needing two trainers to resource the programme. She was, however, very pleased that she had been assertive in renegotiating with David about this.

Internal v. external consultancy

One of the points that arose from our review discussion with Alison was the difference between the position of internal consultants, who are a part of the total client system, and external consultants, who clearly are not.[2] Alison felt that operating as a profit-centre increased her sense of independence, but that she had become aware, even on this first consulting assignment, of how much she felt constrained by the organizational politics. This led us to compare the advantages and disadvantages of internal and external consultants.

The internal consultant

Advantages
- Knows the system (formally and informally) and how to use it.
- Knows the language and how to express ideas in an accepted way.
- May know the key people and how to influence them.
- May have a well-established network of contacts.
- May already have a lot of information about the problem.
- Can work unobtrusively at times.
- Is well placed to seize opportunities.
- Is less likely to be expected to provide instant solutions than the external consultant.
- Can keep in close touch with the longer-term consequences of a project.

Disadvantages
- May have difficulty establishing credibility and indeed visibility.
- Has a history which may get in the way – past failures, old allegiances.
- May be too much part of the system – not sufficiently detached. Indeed may be part of the problem.
- May be *seen* to be too much part of the system, thus limiting trust.
- May feel wary of confronting, especially senior managers.
- May be subject to political/hierarchical pressures.
- May have limited room for manoeuvre because of tight role definitions.
- May not be able to refuse projects.

The external consultant

Advantages
- Is more likely to be seen as outside the politics of the organization.
- People are more likely to be open.
- People may be more willing to listen to and hear this 'outsider'.
- Can bring new perspectives and fresh insights.
- Can more easily provide contacts with other organizations.
- Can become an important communication channel, especially upwards.
- Likely to have high visibility because of people's heightened expectations.
- Can more easily be direct and confronting.
- Has freedom to turn down an assignment.

Disadvantages
- May be 'put on a pedestal', leading to deference/resentment/disillusionment.
- May need a lot of time to discover how the system *really* works.
- May only see part of the problem.
- Leaves at the end of a project and may not see the longer-term results.
- May use ideas which are too different from the organization's current way of thinking.

In assessing these lists we reached two conclusions. First, we recognized that internal and external consultants working together have the potential to be a highly effective partnership if they make conscious use of the benefits of each other's position and help each other overcome the drawbacks. Secondly, we came to believe that internal consultants were likely to be more effective if, as far as possible, they managed themselves and their client relationships as though they were external. In effect, they had to become aware 'outsiders' working on the inside. This role meant monitoring closely the use of their time and its cost-effectiveness; negotiating wants and offers, not only with clients, but with bosses and colleagues as well; assessing the validity and development nature of assignments; striving to occupy a position that was not too firmly fixed in the company's hierarchical structure, but allowed maximum freedom of access; and acquiring the discipline of regularly stepping back from organizational politics, and balancing political sense and independence of mind and action.

This chapter has illustrated the work of the training consultant by following Alison Wright's progress on a single assignment. It is interesting that as soon as she became involved in designing a training intervention for a client manager she came closer to having to deal with 'live' organizational issues rather than stay with the relatively safer simulations of general training courses. It was noticeable that she felt far less comfortable handling the session on the course when the graduates discussed the induction programme with the personnel manager. This called for Alison to act far more in the roles of facilitator, mediator or process consultant than trainer. In the next two chapters we discuss the further development someone like her would need to undertake.

Notes

1   Peters, T. and Austin, N. *A Passion for Excellence*, Collins 1985.
2   For further reading on the differences between internal and external consultants see Swartz, D.H. 'Similarities and Differences of Internal and External Consultants', *Journal of European Industrial Training*, Vol. 4, No. 5, 1975.

6 From training to learning

Introduction

Some organizations find that the combination of general training courses and training consultancy provides the right mix of flexibility and continuity for their management development needs. Others are finding that this approach is not sufficient. Some are caught in a series of dilemmas that have forced a radical revision of their development activities, as is well illustrated by the problems facing the European management development manager of an expanding microchip technology company:

It is a well-established pattern that after an initial period of growth and tremendous flexibility, organizations often settle into more closely defined structures and procedures as a way of controlling the extra complexities that sheer size has brought. There's a plateau period of consolidation. We believe as a company that our survival depends on us not doing this, on our ability to keep up the momentum of change and growth. We're facing enormous challenges. We need to keep recruiting an ever higher calibre of employee from an apparently shrinking pool of talent. We need our staff to be repeatedly changing their skill areas as we introduce new systems to manage the systems we already have. As we expand, we are also removing whole layers of management, merging functions and reshaping the organiz-ation so that people's roles and jobs are being constantly redefined. As a result, the demand for training is soaring. Responding to this at face value means we are engaging in a race we cannot win. We simply are unable to design and run training courses fast enough to meet the rate of change in people's development needs. Training is in danger of becoming a brake on our progress.

Compare this with the problems facing the head of trainer training at a very different kind of company, one of the clearing banks:

We are at an impasse at the moment as long as we keep on thinking in terms of running training courses in the traditional way, no matter how well designed. More and more demands are being placed on Branches and Areas to exercise greater responsi-bility for meeting targets in a more competitive market place and with tighter resources. The demand for staff development is therefore increasing just at a time when there is less willingness to release people for training.

These two examples illustrate the practical problems that force development specialists to question their operating assumptions and pursue fresh lines of enquiry:

- How can we develop people without sending them on training courses?
- How can we make training productive in terms of oper-ational tasks?
- How can we share with managers more of the responsibility for training?
- How can we get people to train each other and them-selves?

- How can we deal with different training needs simultaneously?

Organizations have been experimenting with a variety of methods which provide some solutions to these questions. These fall into five main categories which we will outline briefly.

Distance learning methods

These methods are experiments in bringing development to employees instead of the other way round. They are also ways of multiplying and distributing development resources which are far less costly than the specialized staff needed for face-to-face training. They include video, audio and computer packages, national broadcasts, programmed learning texts, reading material, computer networking and correspondence courses, as well as tapping the expanding resources of the World Wide Web. In some companies the development function sees itself operating as a mini 'open college'.

Self-directed learning workshops

Where courses are still considered an important part of development activities, companies are dealing with a diverse set of development needs on the same programme by including designs in which course members work on their different learning goals by drawing on the resources available. We have heard this described as the 'play-school' approach, where a diversity of needs and resources are mixed and matched in creative ways in a joint undertaking between course leaders and course members.

Action learning sets

This widely used approach was developed originally by Reg Revans. Small groups of managers meet regularly as a 'set' with the help of a set adviser to work on the tasks and problems facing each member. Instead of running a number of courses with one group of course members after another, a set adviser may be working with many different sets, each of which may meet for maybe one day a month. In a sense 'courses' are thus scattered in space and time throughout the organization, dealing with the actual development needs of managers as they arise, with the set advisers helping to create and catalyse the conditions in which these problem-solving 'cells' can thrive.

Self-development groups

More loosely structured groups than action learning sets, they are less primarily task-focused, where members can identify, explore and work on their development needs. The boundaries of this exploration may be closely or widely defined. Work, domestic, practical, emotional, task and personal issues may be addressed. This approach is often seen as a seeding process on the part of the development function. The groups may be formed on courses as syndicate groups or 'support and challenge groups' that continue to meet after the programme. Development specialists may actively start a number of such groups by putting people in touch with one another and helping the groups to establish ways of working together which will enable them to become self-sustaining. These ideas are also informing some team-building approaches.

Developing managers as developers

Some organizations are giving this area priority for investing their development resources. The skill and expertise needed for developing people becomes one of the core competences for general line management, instead of residing in a separate specialist function. This function is then staffed not with developers, but with developers of developers whose tasks then become:

1   Designing ways of developing this new core competence. (Paradoxically this sometimes is seen as running a whole new breed of training courses for managers.)
2   Designing procedures and resources to support managers in their role as developers.

The nature of this development path

In Chapter 4 we discussed the development path from training to consulting in terms of new demands placed on trainers to learn how to develop collaborative relationships with client managers. We suggested that this required a qualitatively different way of working which trainers may not necessarily have acquired.

Although it might appear that trainers or training consultants could take on the new activities outlined above relatively easily, we have seen again and again that unless people understand their work in terms of learning rather than training, then the new activities are unsuccessful. Initiatives begun with optimism peter out. New approaches fail somehow to take hold in the organization. Distance learning packages are made widely available, but turn out to be scarcely used; the membership of action learning sets tails off; self-development group meetings degenerate into social events and then cease altogether; participants and leaders on self-directed learning workshops end up frustrated and dissatisfied, vaguely blaming one another for expectations that have not been met; managers attend courses on developing staff and then return to work and nominate their staff for other courses.

One common cause of these problems is that wider organizational issues are not being considered. We shall address this point when we look at the third development path in Chapter 8.

The second cause is that the development specialists responsible for initiating these projects have not developed a learning-based approach. They are doing learning-based activities with a training-based orientation and training-based skills and techniques. The change from developing people to enabling their self-development calls for a fundamental shift in values, aims and approach. To uncover these we shall now look at the principles underlying what is variously called self-motivated learning, self-directed learning or management self-development, and which we are referring to as learning-based approaches. These are:

1   People can only choose to learn; they cannot be made to learn.
2   All activities are opportunities for learning.
3   Different people learn in different ways.
4   People who have learned how to learn are the best equipped to deal with continuous change.
5   Learning is a journey, not a destination.

People can only choose to learn; they cannot be made to learn

To understand the significance of this principle we need to differentiate learning, as we use the term, from what is more aptly termed memorizing. People can memorize knowledge, behaviour and attitudes, storing for later use what others have taught or shown them. This capacity is very useful for rapid adaptation. A large amount of childhood socialization is acquired in this way and traditionally our education system has compounded this further.

Memorizing has particular characteristics. The material is swallowed whole, added to an individual's store and reproduced when the appropriate trigger is activated, either by conscious choice or unconsciously because of a stimulus in the environment. Neither the memorizer nor the material is fundamentally changed in the process, although the material may be distorted by the memorizer's own filter.

Learning is quite different. New material is assimilated by being thoroughly chewed and digested; then unwanted bits are rejected. The learner thus changes the material and is changed by it. This is the dynamic process of learning.

Going back to the principle we are discussing, it is possible to see how people can memorize things almost passively. But fully integrated learning requires of the learner a highly active, discriminating involvement.

Training courses are often geared more to memorizing than to learning. Trainees memorize concepts and information when they attend effective presentations with good visual aids. Training films reinforce the points in memorable ways, using graphics, humour or dramatic devices. Trainers design exercises for course members to practise and become familiar with certain skills and techniques; they may demonstrate and model behaviours for trainees to copy. The concern of many trainers is the decay over time of this kind of 'learning' and the need for immediate application and reinforcement at work.

Undoubtedly integrated learning also takes place on training courses; the more participative the training, the more opportunity there is for this to happen. However, most trainers and course members are comfortable and familiar with a balance of responsibility that is weighted towards the trainer. Course members may expect to work hard, but there is a tendency for all parties to underestimate how strong is the expectation that people will be told what to learn, how to learn and how successfully they have learned.

The most important aspect of this first principle, then, is the shift towards far greater learner responsibility for the development process. With a learning approach, the involvement of learners in every stage of the development process is not just desirable, but all-important, because their motivation and commitment are paramount. Such an approach presents difficulties for trainers on the training to learning development path. It means that those treading it must:

- Review how truly self-responsible they are being for their own development. If they are avoiding this, they will certainly fail in their attempts to enable others to become more self-responsible.
- Learn to recognize the many ways in which others avoid or struggle with taking on greater self-responsibility.
- Learn to intervene helpfully at these points without taking back all the responsibility.

These needs are just the beginning. Those pursuing this path find themselves grappling with many difficult questions that force them to reappraise their values and sense of purpose. Consider the following:

- If I accept that individuals should identify their own development needs, do I accept all those needs as valid in the business context? If not, on what basis do I make the distinction? Is it up to me to make the distinction?

- How much do I believe I know what is best for people? How much of my self-esteem is tied up with people wanting to be dependent on my help? What sort of help should I be giving? What is 'help'?
- If I see people not facing up to their responsibilities, is it because they do not want to or because they do not understand what this means? What is my responsibility in this?
- If people put pressure on me to teach them the 'right' answers, how do I respond? What are the consequences?

What distinguishes training specialists from learning specialists is their willingness to struggle with these complex issues, without paralysing themselves, even though such questions can never be finally resolved.

All activities are opportunities for learning

Alan Mumford[1] has referred to 'informal managerial development' as the haphazard process whereby managers learn as they are promoted, change jobs, handle crises and work with different people. Management development specialists have traditionally sought to organize this otherwise chance process by succession planning, secondments and special projects. The idea is to give managers opportunities to acquire certain experience and skills at particular times in their careers, in a way that benefits both the individuals and the organization. This approach to management development seeks to control and manage learning opportunities as instruments for meeting anticipated business requirements. The emphasis is on the end result of the learning, the new knowledge and skills which managers can bring to their work. In this sense, the learning process itself is merely the vehicle for improved task achievement.

The shift in perception inherent in a learning-based approach is threefold. First, there needs to be a recognition that *all* organizational tasks can be a source of conscious, self-directed learning by managers. Secondly comes the ability to set learning goals *and* task achievement goals for all activities. Thirdly, learning and task achievement become vitally interdependent, neither one merely the vehicle for the other.

The development need on the training to learning path is a considerable increase in creativity for:

- Recognizing developmental resources.
- Realizing the opportunities for learning inherent in situations.
- Designing task achievement/learning opportunities.
- Releasing the creative energy in others that will fuel self-motivated development.

Different people learn in different ways

We now have a substantial body of knowledge about the nature of adult learning. The work of David Kolb[2] has been influential in identifying four stages in the process of learning (Figure 6.1).

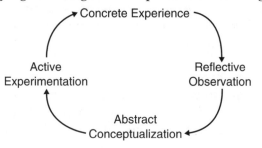

Figure 6.1   Kolb's learning cycle

His research showed that it is rare for individuals to give equal emphasis to all four stages. People have learning preferences which determine the ease or difficulty with which they are able to learn from different kinds of experiences. Brain research has shown that people can organize information in different ways. Left-brain thinking is largely analytical and logical, right-brain thinking is more intuitive and holistic. People differ even in the way they take in information through their senses. Neuro-linguistic programming suggests that people are differentially attuned to visual, auditory and kinaes-thetic stimuli.

Professionals interested in both training and learning draw on this information, but they tend to use it in different ways. A training approach which concentrates on the competences people acquire as the end result of training uses adult learning theory *implicitly* to design training courses to suit a range of learning preferences. The aim is to create situations in which people can acquire new knowledge and skills rapidly. A learning approach uses learning theory *explicitly* to help managers understand:

- How people learn.
- How learning can be blocked.
- Their own strengths and weaknesses as learners.
- How to create conditions for maximizing the strengths of their own learning style.
- How to build new strengths as learners.
- How to become more aware of collective patterns in the culture and structure of the organization which may support or inhibit learning.

Not only do people learn in different ways, what they learn will be unique to each individual. Training seeks to help people arrive at more or less the same end point whereas individual learning will be diverse and cannot be defined in advance in the same way as training objectives.

The development need along the training to learning path is to become thoroughly conversant with theories and models about the nature of adult learning and to be able to impart this understanding to managers in ways they can use for their own and others' development.

People who have learned how to learn are the best equipped to deal with continuous change

This principle provides the rationale for the learning approach in today's business world. In stable conditions organizations develop a set of operating norms which remain valid over time.

To be successful, single loop learning is sufficient. The term comes from cybernetics, the study of artificial intelligence, and describes a simple negative feedback system which enables self-regulation in steady state conditions. (See Figure 6.2.)

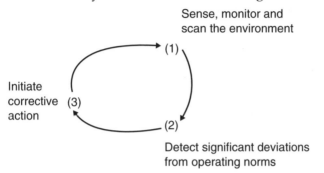

Sense, monitor and scan the environment

(1)

Initiate corrective (3) action

(2)

Detect significant deviations from operating norms

Figure 6.2   Single loop learning

Double loop learning is required for self-regulation in turbulent times. It is so called because a second loop is drawn to represent the extra level of 'intelligence' needed to question the operating norms themselves. (See Figure 6.3.)

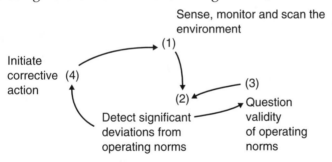

Sense, monitor and scan the environment

(1)

Initiate corrective (4) action

(2)

(3)

Question validity of operating norms

Detect significant deviations from operating norms

Figure 6.3   Double loop learning

This difference is similar to that between 'learning' and 'learning to learn'. The latter mode requires people to challenge and change their goals and tasks as circumstances evolve by recognizing and questioning the underlying assumptions on which these are based. This autonomous, flexible, proactive approach to managing at work is best matched by a learning-based approach to development which is more likely to foster exactly these qualities in people.

The development need for those seeking to use this approach in management development is to understand how to set up the conditions in which learning to learn can flourish. Gareth Morgan[3] suggests that this involves three key areas:

1   Acknowledging legitimate error as a source of learning of great practical value. Encouraging people to be open about and interested in mistakes and uncertainties.
2   Encouraging the exploration of difference and allowing constructive conflict and debate between competing perspectives. Encouraging the redefinition and reframing of problems instead of rushing straight into solutions.
3   Balancing people's need for structure and guidance with an appropriate level of autonomy and flexibility in the development process. Traditionally this has been achieved by defining fixed goals and objectives and allowing freedom in the choice of methods for achieving the desired outcomes. A deeper level of responsible autonomy is achieved by exploring and defining the constraints within which freedom of choice and action can be exercised. This means people identify for themselves goals *and* methods which are compatible with an agreed system of company values.

Learning is a journey, not a destination

The truism of rapid and continuous change makes it almost inevitable that people's knowledge and skills need to be rapidly and continuously upgraded. However, even without this, there is always more to learn; as one question is answered, others will be immediately raised. An example is where 360° feedback is used. Recipients often go into this exercise expecting that everything will become clear; that their strengths and development needs will be identified. Whilst this clarity is sometimes present, other confusions arise at the same time: differences of view between the givers of the feedback; apparently contradictory views, even from the same person; some vagueness, as well as possibly the totally unexpected. As a result the 360°

feedback raises many subjects for exploration. This can be frustrating. The plea often heard at this point is, 'I can't start learning until I know what I have to work on'. The mind shift needed is to recognize that the learning has already begun through the act of trying to find out what to work on and the act of trying to find out what to work on is in itself probably the most relevant point to learn. While there are many virtues in the more systematic and analytical approaches to learning as typified in the training cycle (see p. 42), an equally powerful case can be made for the humanistic tradition. This is based upon the assumptions first, that the world presents us with incidents and experiences which tell us what we need to learn; and if we do not learn we will be constantly reminded of it. Second, that at whatever point we embark upon the journey then that is, by definition, the right place.

After elaborating these five principles, we are now in a position to extract some important differences between an approach to development based on training and one based on learning:

Training	*Learning*
Training is an instrument for improving task achievement.	Learning is an all-important goal, alongside task achievement.
Training often means memorizing the new.	Learning always means assimilating the new.
Trainees do not necessarily need to understand *how* they learn.	It is essential for learners to become aware of and actively manage their own learning.
Learning theory is used implicitly to design efficient training.	Learning theory is used explicitly to enable self-development.
Responsibility for training rests with the trainer. Trainee involvement in setting training objectives, choosing training methods and deciding how to evaluate them is not essential.	Responsibility for learning rests with the learner. His/her involvement in all aspects of the development process is vital.

| The desired outcomes of training are the same for all individuals. | The outcomes of learning are unique to each individual. |
| Prepares people for a known future. | Prepares people for an unknown future. |

In this chapter we have tried to show that trainers cannot be expected to adopt learning-based approaches overnight. In order to become competent in this field they need above all to engage in their own self-development. Inevitably this will be a different route for every individual trainer but those who would like some practical ideas for getting started will find a self-development plan in Appendix I and should also refer to Suggested Reading.

Just as trainers cannot be expected to adopt learning-based approaches overnight, neither can their clients. A manager wanting a two-day change management course is likely to be irritated if the trainer pushes for a totally different approach. No matter how creative or versatile the options the consultant may offer, they are of no value if the client cannot see the relevance. So clients may well need to be *weaned* away from training to learning, by being offered the unknown but in the context of the known, e.g. a two-day course part of which is a self-directed workshop (see Appendix II).

In the next chapter we look at the work of learning consultants, who combine competences gained from two development paths, that of training to consulting and training to learning. The two paths are mutually reinforcing in many ways, so that experience gained in one is helpful for the other. For example, consulting experience requires good contracting skills, which are needed for negotiating learning contracts with managers. Similarly the interdependence of development goals and business goals in learning-based approaches makes for practical and productive consultancy.

Notes

1 Mumford, A. 'Using Reality in Management Development', *Management Education and Development*, Vol. 18, No. 3, 1987.
2 Kolb, D.A., Rubin, I.M. and McIntyre, J.M. *Organizational Psychology – an Experiential Approach*, Prentice-Hall 1974.
3 Morgan, G. *Images of Organization*, Sage 1997.

7 The learning consultant

In the previous chapter we quoted a training manager concerned about the way that his organization handled the development of people. He believed that the members of his training team had too much of a course mentality; he wanted them to see their role in much wider terms. He talked about them becoming developers rather than trainers; using the nomenclature we have introduced in this book, it became clear that he wanted them to operate more as learning consultants. This chapter describes our work with that team.

A learning consultancy assignment

Early stages of the project
The team's current approach matched the expectations of participants and the generally bureaucratic nature of the organization, but it was not developmental. Managers and staff took very little responsibility for themselves, reinforcing a culture that was inimical to success in the newly competitive environment of the financial world. There was not as yet a

climate in which self-motivated learning (our client's term) could flourish.

We needed to stimulate the team's thinking about their manager's vision of a radically different way of working. Since it was some time before the total group could meet, we recorded our initial discussion about the desired future on videotape, distributed it to the team members and asked them to respond in whatever way they wanted.

We learned a lot from this mistake. As individuals watched the video on their own, they were nonplussed and fearful of new and apparently enormous demands suddenly being placed on them. They had not contributed to the formulation of the vision and, far from being inspired, they were appalled, and responded in ways characteristic of the organization's culture. There was no outspoken rejection but a series of passively resistant ploys: silence, procrastination, evasion, bland comments, dutiful noises and a series of 'yes, but . . .' responses.

We realized that we had made a leap too far ahead of our clients' starting point. We had not set up the conditions for change in terms of the 'Gleicher formula',[1] which states that for change to occur $A \times B \times C > D$ where A is dissatisfaction with the present, B is desire for a new situation, C is awareness of the first practical steps and D is the cost of change, emotional as well as practical and financial. At this stage the team were simply counting the cost to themselves of adopting a very different way of working.

At this point we returned to a more structured approach in formulating our proposals for a working contract:

- To increase A (dissatisfaction with the present) we decided to encourage debate about the effectiveness of the current training approach in the light of the organization's future needs. We distributed reading materials and questions that would develop a wider perspective and curiosity from the team about the trends of change and their particular implications for training and development in the organization.
- To develop B (desire for a new situation) we offered a variety of ways that we could work with the team in their

transition that would help them to experience, understand and, we hoped, become excited by different approaches to development (see Figure 7.1).

- To clarify C (awareness of first steps) we needed to identify possible interim stages that the team could move through in developing towards learning consultant roles (see Figure 7.2).

---

1   **Team-building:** helping the team as a whole to develop.
2   **Joint research:** to identify development needs within the organization and to assess the impact of new and existing training and development interventions.
3   **Design workshops:** helping the team members develop an innovative approach in designing new programmes and revitalizing existing ones.
4   **Co-leading:** on new programmes or activities where internal expertise is being developed or on external programmes arranged by the consultants.
5   **Development contracts:** through intensive small group tutorials and practice sessions or on a distance learning basis through audio- and videotape.
6   **Counselling:** on an *ad hoc* basis or as part of a series of personal development sessions.
7   **Resource link:** providing information and advice on training and development activities and arranging contacts with other organizations.
8   **Co-consulting:** helping trainers make the transition towards a consultancy role within their own organization.

Figure 7.1   Options for using the external consultants

Developing a working contract

Our proposal suggested three phases for what became known as the Joint Development Project:

1   Interviews with team members, followed by some guided reading and exchange of comments by audiotape. At this point members would be asked if they were willing to make a provisional commitment to the project. On that basis they

PRESENT TRAINERS 1	INTERIM STAGES 2	3	4	FUTURE DEVELOPERS 5
Runs standard courses in standard ways, to meet generalized training needs. Expects participants to reach the same end point. Takes responsibility for what happens on programmes and evaluates outcomes. Is mainly concerned with content.	Offers options within standard courses which allow participants to meet particular needs which arise within the programme aims. Helps people identify individual needs and select learning methods. Coordinates activities. Higher process concern.	Offers programmes within which there is considerable time for self-directed activities. Pre-course work with participants identifies needs and prepares for the course. Accepts that outcomes may vary widely within the aims of the programme. Helps people learn about learning and self-management.	Programme is jointly designed by total group when it comes together, after extensive pre-work. Everybody shares expertise and resources. 'Developer' manages the boundary and affirms the values and methods of self-managed learning and mutual development. Undertakes extensive follow-up. High level of process and task concern.	Negotiates long-term development contracts with individuals and groups. People engage in a variety of learning activities separately and together. Goals are continuously renewed and extended. Wide variety of roles including teacher, coach, mentor, counsellor, resource investigator, process consultant.

Figure 7.2   Learning consultant roles

would then engage in an initial stocktake of their current knowledge and skills and begin identifying needs. They would design this activity themselves calling on us as necessary.

2   A workshop for all members of the team and their manager. The purpose of this event would be to:
  (a) Review the current work of the team and team relationships.
  (b) Clarify roles and expectations regarding the Joint Development Project, including issues of resourcing and support.
  (c) Review the findings of the self- and peer-assessment and its implications for individual and team development.
  (d) Test commitment to participating further in the project.

3   Implementation of the development plans. Each member would have an agreed number of consultant days to draw on in assisting her or his development. They could join forces where needs were shared so as to use less consultant time. The principle was that they would be responsible for deciding when and how to use us as resources, to be as creative as possible in making the best use of us and to stretch us as much as we would aim to stretch them.

We identified a number of necessary conditions for the success of the project. These were:

- A clear understanding of the values, rationale and practical implications of self-motivated learning.
- A willingness by all to help each member of the team identify specific goals, together with means of measuring progress towards them.
- A shared commitment to offer support and challenge.
- Clarity about how much freedom each person really had in moving towards their developmental goals. Open discussion and negotiation about this.
- A willingness to try out different methods of learning.

- A willingness to bring back learning to the team and to build on one another's work.
- A willingness for each person only to make agreements they were really committed to.

This proposal was accepted by the team. In effect we had negotiated the kind of long-term development contract with them that they would themselves be setting up in future with their own internal clients.

Review of implementation

We went ahead with phases one and two of the proposal and then held a review with our client, the training manager. We felt that so far our design had been basically sound. We had modelled learning consultancy rather than training in a number of ways:

- During the workshop we gave no formal theory inputs, but simple models and ideas arising from phase (1) work were posted round the room at the outset as resources for all of us.
- A variety of books and other learning materials were available for participants to use whenever they wished.
- We regularly discussed and renegotiated our role with the group.
- We used the changes in our relationship with the group as a way of illustrating different training and consultant roles.
- We worked explicitly at the levels of task, procedures and process.
- We worked with the group's external boundaries (its new relationships with the rest of the organization) and its internal boundaries (the working relationships between team members and with the manager).

We were not satisfied at this point that we had resolved one difficult aspect of the group, which was indicative of the organization's culture as a whole – the tendency already mentioned for people to go along with things on the surface but then passively sabotage them by losing momentum. People were immensely skilful at providing the required response in a situation (including the apparent acceptance of self-responsibility!). They were accustomed to a basically dependent relationship with anyone they perceived to be in authority and our engagement by their manager as consultants was sufficient for us to be seen in such a role. They were keen and constructive in public, and floundered when left to continue working independently. Despite much discussion and negotiation (in hindsight a futile tactic), we knew the team remained dependent on external motivation. This block was right at the heart of any development towards a learning consultancy approach by the team.

We had also learned by this stage that the team members did not have a great deal of insight into their own behaviour and feelings. They lacked information about ways in which they could impede their own development or that of others, having had little exposure to any form of personal, as opposed to professional, development. They had found the process of self- and peer-assessment difficult to design or engage in, so that their initial learning goals were vague and relatively superficial. It was clear that they lacked the process skills so necessary for consultancy such as:

- Highly tuned listening and observation skills for picking up the process level in group interaction or individual communication.
- Making 'here and now' interventions that worked explicitly or implicitly with the process level.
- Timing interventions, judging when to speak or act and when to remain silent.
- The capacity to give simple, direct feedback.

We believed that confronting the self-responsibility issues head on would be counter-productive. We decided we needed to redesign the next stages in order to:

- Provide opportunities for personal development.
- Transfer the tendency to meet others' expectations from the

context of authority relationships (real or perceived) to a peer level.

- Remove individuals from the over-comfortable cohesiveness that seemed to take over when the team was working together.
- Provide sufficient support for individuals to feel more inclined to explore the areas of freedom open to them, rather than huddle defensively together in the centre of the field of play.

Redesign of the project

As a result of the review we agreed some structures in which the further identification and implementation of individual and team development plans could take place. A system of mentoring and a self- and mutual development group were created.

The mentoring was based on a contract between pairs within the team and one external consultant. The three worked closely together, and within this safer and yet challenging relationship the danger of compliance was reduced. We realize that we have rather distorted the definition of organizational mentor, which usually refers to a more experienced manager taking a less experienced manager under his or her wing and offering both practical and emotional help: encouragement in undertaking new assignments, role modelling, sponsorship, counselling and friendship. Clearly this can only take place when both parties belong to the same organization; however, we felt that the word mentor still best described the flavour of the relationship.

The development group was directly related to the mentoring. It was made up of all members of the team, plus one of the mentors as facilitator at each meeting. The group provided a setting for:

1 Discussion of the progress individuals were making.
2 Skill development.
3 Discussing various training and consultancy problems.
4 Giving and receiving feedback.
5 Reviewing learning about the nature of self-development

and planning ways in which this could be transferred to the team's work with organizational clients.

One of the outcomes of this phase of the project was an improvement in the relationship between the training manager and his team. Although his vision and enthusiasm were appreciated he had been seen as inconsistent in his style, sometimes taking a low profile and relying on his staff to use their initiative, then suddenly getting 'cold feet' and intervening with numerous demands. The development group was able to start establishing its own boundaries, to the point of giving the manager some clear feedback on what was helpful and unhelpful about the ways he managed them. The mentoring and the time in the development group were important for building this sort of confidence and autonomy, bearing in mind the extent of deference in the organization.

Final review and closure

In reviewing the project as a whole the manager and the team were satisfied that they had made considerable progress towards working more as learning consultants. They now saw themselves as being in the third and fourth columns of Figure 7.2:

- The number of standard courses was substantially reduced in favour of consulting assignments.
- There were few isolated training events; most courses were supported by extensive pre- and post-course work.
- There was far greater responsibility being placed on the learner.
- A number of distance learning packages were prepared.
- The level of motivation in the team was higher.
- Other groups of trainers in the organization approached this team for help in taking more of a learning consultant approach to their work.

There were a number of other aspects which we felt worthy of note.

Despite the innovations mentioned above there were still a number of standard training courses to be run. The training manager was keen to avoid a sharp division between the trainers and the learning consultants, and established two groups, but without fixed membership. The learning consultant group was made up of people temporarily seconded from the training group; it had a leader who was responsible for overseeing all projects, but who would also in time return to training. The importance of cross-fertilization between the two groups was regarded as vital. One way of doing this was the institution of a project book into which any member of the whole group could write suggestions for areas of the team's work which would benefit from a learning consultancy approach. The whole team would hold regular meetings to decide which projects should be taken on.

An important impetus for team growth was the need to educate client managers about the changing approach and to negotiate with other groups of trainers in the organization. In planning and implementing their strategy the team members were also acquiring some important consultancy skills. Having a newcomer join the team half-way through the project proved to be invaluable; she was curious and intelligent. As an outsider she was able to ask lots of naïve questions which caused people to rethink what they were doing. In order for her to be successfully inducted, members of the team had to explain to her their understanding of the project and how it was progressing. The training manager now sees movement into and out of the team as helping it to 'keep its cutting edge'; it is forced regularly to reappraise what it is doing and the values which underpin its work.

The training manager now believes, and we agree with him, that we should have pushed him earlier to be more open with his own boss about his plans. We should have stressed the necessity for him to collaborate with his boss and indeed other parts of the organization as the various changes became apparent. As consultants we had colluded with somebody who saw himself as going out on a limb, allowing a somewhat covert start to the project and risking exactly the isolation that our client feared.

What makes this project an example of learning consultancy is the way the contract was limited to the development of the individual trainers and the team as a whole. The scope of the assignment did not allow us to address more explicitly the wider organizational culture. This extension of the project would have taken us into the field of organization change consultancy which is the subject of the next two chapters.

Note

1   Sheane, D. 'Organization Development in Action', *Journal of European Industrial Training*, Vol. 2, No. 8, 1978.

8 From individual change to organizational change

The two development paths already described require trainers to increase their understanding of the nature of consulting relationships and of adult learning and self-development. The third path encompasses both of these and goes further in two ways:

1   The capacity to work with the change and development of larger systems: from a single individual to a work group, to a larger unit of interlinked groups, to a whole organization and to systems of organizations such as the subsidiaries in a multinational company.
2   The capacity to meet this greater complexity with cognitive maps both rich enough and simple enough to guide understanding and action in enabling change.

The nature of this development path

We have found that although some people may set out to work with organizational change as the goal of their development, many emerge somewhere along this third path as a consequence of cumulative experience as trainers, training consultants or learning consultants. Often these are people who start to recognize trends in their work, and by focusing on these more directly they begin to accelerate their development. We look at how this can happen in each case.

Training experience

The evolution here occurs when trainers recognize that people *change* in becoming more competent. Odd as it may seem, many trainers do not see their work in these terms. They regard training as 'giving managers more tools for their kit bag'. The new ideas, techniques and approaches that participants are introduced to on courses stay firmly instrumental. There is a collusive element at work here which allows everyone to avoid the potentially disturbing possibility of personal change, in favour of a non-threatening rationalization, whereby participants leave with some extra bits and pieces at their disposal, but remain fundamentally untouched themselves. With this frame of reference, problems only arise if the tools on offer are not relevant to participants or if they are not clearly understood; in either case the implication is that the trainer's research or presentation is at fault.

The more trainers engage with participants before, during and after courses, the less adequate this approach is likely to seem. Trainers discover how very differently people perceive the same experience; how difficult the application of certain ideas and behaviours will be for some; how resistant one person might be to seeing any value in an approach that another seizes with alacrity. It becomes apparent to trainers that they are dealing with a whole range of non-rational responses to the possibility of personal readjustment. They see the need to understand how people change and to develop refined skills and insights for intervening helpfully in this process. They may turn to psychology for theories based on behavioural, psycho-analytical or humanistic schools of thought, and to the professional field of counselling and therapy for practical application.

As they progress more deeply in working with individual change, their own and others', they may also feel the need to reflect more rigorously on their own role in organizations. They will need to consider how best they can transfer experience gained in a very personal therapeutic context to a business environment without violating ethical and practical consider-ations. They will decide how implicitly or explicitly they will address personal change issues. They will realize that there are many influences for change shaping each individual, and that people cannot be understood separately from their environment.

In this way training experience in itself may draw someone on to our third development path, in the search for a deeper understanding of individual change in organizational settings.

Consulting experience

An evolution in thinking occurs as consultants stop seeing each project undertaken with a different client manager as a self-contained assignment and start to recognize the links in their work. Finding themselves closer to the realities of the business world, they see the neat formulations which sufficed in the training room give way before the greater complexity of the live situation. They are faced with untangling a number of inter-related variables and find it increasingly difficult to distinguish cause and effect. In order to contract effectively for any one assignment they need to recognize a network of organization links, both formal and informal. As they consult with working units rather than train collections of individuals, they discover the need to be concerned as much with the boundary between the unit and the rest of the organization, as with internal group dynamics.

As a result of this experience, consultants become interested in the wider context of their work instead of defining it purely in terms of designing development for a particular group. They draw their working boundaries ever more inclusively as they move from a closed-system to an open-system perspective, introducing them to the fields of organizational behaviour and

organization development and various approaches for understanding and planning large-scale organizational change.

Experience with learning-based approaches

It is impossible to develop an appreciation of adult learning
and management self-development without dealing with the
nature of personal change. In addition, learning consultants
focus particularly on creating the *conditions* in which others
define and pursue their development goals. As they work with
different groups of people in the organization, they help to set
up mini-cultures in which learning and self-development can
flourish. Such mini-cultures include developmental resources,
processes, relationships and policies.

Inevitably, these cultures will be limited and temporary, if
consultants do not start working with the wider organizational
culture and its impact in inhibiting or facilitating different kinds
of learning. Once they begin to work with managers to make
explicit the cultural norms of the organization and to understand how these are maintained and changed, consultants find
themselves working with the dynamics of collective learning.
They become interested in concepts such as 'the learning organization' and 'organizational culture', and once again become
aware that they are on the development path from individual
to organizational change.

Comparison with organization development

So far we have looked at the ways people may develop towards
organization change consulting from a background in individual management development. It is interesting at this point
to see how organization development (OD) has evolved as a
profession from its emergence in the 1960s, since it is an
approach which has always set out to encompass the whole
organization.

Organization development grew from the application of the
behavioural sciences to organizations. It embraced humanistic
principles, which counter-balanced the more scientific and

mechanistic models of organizational functioning. Just when the idea of continuous change was emerging as the given context in which organizations would have to operate, OD offered the possibility of 'managing' change by implementing long-term, coordinated and highly systematic interventions.

In 1969 Richard Beckhard[1] defined OD as 'an effort which is *planned*, *organization-wide*, and *managed* from the *top*, to increase *organization effectiveness* and *health* through interventions based on *behavioural-science* knowledge'. The profession developed a wealth of intervention strategies, a whole technology of change based primarily on:

- Working with *groups* as the basic building blocks of an organization.
- Working on *intergroup* relationships between subsystems.
- Working on *planning* and *goal-setting* processes.
- Working on *educational* activities for upgrading the knowledge, skill and abilities of *key* personnel.

Fifteen years or so after Beckhard was writing, Adrian McLean[2] et al. undertook research into OD as it was *actually* being practised and concluded that the profession had evolved in a number of ways. In summary these were:

1 Far less emphasis on applying well-developed theories and techniques of change; more emphasis on consultants developing their own ideas and approaches to meet each new situation.
2 Less ambitious organization-wide programmes; more emphasis on the cumulative effect of smaller projects undertaken over time.
3 Fewer discrete, finite projects; more continuous and seamless activities.
4 Less evangelism and idealism; more pragmatic acceptance of the political realities of organizational life.
5 Less of the stance of an OD consultant as a neutral, external facilitator towards a more active partiality and involvement in the change process.

6   Less emphasis on *planned* change; more emphasis on *plann-able* change, i.e. the daily task of addressing issues as they arise.
7   Less emphasis on rational, sequential descriptions of the change process; more reliance on intuitive, integrative, holistic understanding of the nature of change.

Further evidence of the route along which OD professionals have developed comes from Robert Tannenbaum and Robert Hanna.[3] Writing about organization change consulting, they identified the lack of emphasis on the *individual* human system in traditional OD work, particularly the individual in transition. 'The nature of any system change and the degree to which it is realized, ultimately depend upon the unique responses of the individuals involved in the change.' They highlight the range of studies into the stages of personal transition which accompany significant life changes and crises, all of which follow some pattern of 'holding on, letting go and moving on'. They point out that OD has concentrated primarily on planning and implementing the 'moving on' stage of change, while dealing with 'resistance to change' in relatively superficial ways. As a result important change programmes have encountered great difficulty in building up momentum and solidly maintaining it over a period of time.

The authors suggest that OD professionals need to pay more attention to understanding the human processes of 'holding on' and facilitating the ability to 'let go', i.e. dealing with the emotional responses to loss and the attempt to avoid the accompanying pain (e.g. shock, frustration, confusion, anger, helplessness and depression). Helping people work through such reactions requires more than a purely systematic behavioural-science approach.

All this bodes well for those seeking to develop towards organization change consultancy. It would appear that in treading the path from individual change to organizational change, they are likely to meet an OD consultant walking the other way. In fact the path turns out not to be a linear journey, as in Figure 8.1. Rather the area we are exploring is the fertile ground where the two perspectives meet and create new possibilities. (See Figure 8.2.)

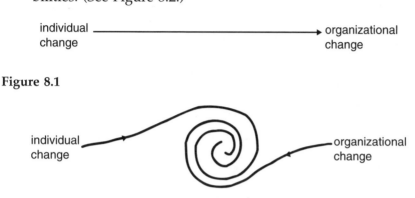

Figure 8.1

Figure 8.2

In Chapter 11 we will explore other ways of understanding the links between individual, local activity and system-wide change. For now we will suggest one way of developing the systemic perspective needed for this development path.

Developing the capacity to work with organizational change

What does it take to work with organizational change over and above the knowledge, skills and attitudes described in earlier chapters? Once consultants can develop strong collaborative relationships with clients, can undertake effectively the necessary work in all stages of the consulting cycle, and can create the conditions for self- and mutual development by enabling managers to learn how to learn, have they acquired all the competences they need? Is the role of change agent in an organization anything more than a flexible combination of the other roles already mentioned? (See Figure 8.3.)

In our experience further development *is* needed and at times the extra step can seem large. Those consultants working with organizational change testify to the intellectual demand of con-

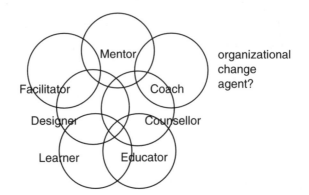

Figure 8.3

ceptualizing about organizations, change and the business world, in ways that can inform practical action.

They also find that to remain creative and responsive in conditions of complex change requires considerable emotional resilience. Finally there is a need for increased autonomy and sense of self based on clarity of purpose and values.

Since this can seem like trying to climb a steep cliff without toe-holds, our suggestion for those with limited experience of organization change consulting is to take a fresh look at their skills in constructing and using models for understanding change. Although such a task might appear to be a purely conceptual activity, it is more demanding than it seems and can be invaluable in developing some important capacities for working with organizational change. This idea is supported by Gordon Lippitt's list of the attributes of the successful modeller:[4]

1   Personal security – the courage and confidence to step back from a complex situation and trust one's ability to construe it in different ways, rather than become paralysed and confused.
2   Situational sensitivity – above-average capacity to tune in to a situation and perceive a large range of factors at work.
3   Judgement – a willingness to add to, discard or amend a model as the situation develops or new information comes to light.

4   Balance of analysis and synthesis – the ability to break down a situation into parts and relate and combine the parts into meaningful, creative wholes.
5   Tolerance of ambiguity – the ability to work with disorder, paradox and uncertainty while continually searching for meaning. The ability to resist pressure for immediate answers or solutions.

If competence in modelling requires these capacities, then it clearly offers a route for development. The following plan illustrates a sequence which has helped many of the people we have worked with:

1   Understand the nature of models.
2   Become conscious of the models, frameworks and principles already underpinning one's current work.
3   Experiment with using familiar models to generate an organizational perspective.
4   Learn about a wider range of organizational models.
5   Create one's own models.

The range of potentially useful models is vast. In the remainder of this chapter we illustrate modelling as a developmental activity rather than attempting any kind of inventory. Our intention is to stimulate the reader's thinking about this approach to developing self or others as organization change consultants.

Understanding the nature of models

We all have cognitive maps which govern the meaning we make of any situation and so enable us to decide on purposeful action. The emphasis here is on the word purposeful. It is possible to leap straight from the experience of a situation into action, but it is the stage of reflection and meaning-making which informs and guides action. For the consultant it is the quality of the meaning-making which underwrites the design of effective change interventions. This is where models come in: 'In simple terms a model is a way of *representing* a complex situation so as to define certain aspects of it and their interrelationships'.[5]

Models are at the heart of the work of the organization change consultant. They enable him or her to:

- *Describe* a complex situation, and highlight where information is needed.
- *Interpret* the situation, through the interrelationships inherent in the model, leading to clearer understanding.
- *Design* ways of intervening in a situation as the model allows assessment of the possible consequences of action.
- *Communicate* with others about the situation and develop shared perceptions.

The consulting cycle referred to in Chapter 4 which isolates seven activities and links them sequentially, i.e. a typical *schematic* model, as is an organization chart which depicts the hierarchical relationships between roles in a company management structure. Models can also be *concrete* (such as the scaled-down replica of a production plant), *abstract* (such as mathematical symbols linked by a formula, e.g. H_2O is an abstract model of water) or *analogous* (such as thinking of an organization as a machine designed to deliver certain products).

It is helpful to recognize that all models are metaphorical, that they suggest a way of seeing that simultaneously makes certain aspects of a situation more visible while blinding the observer to other aspects. For example, as mentioned above, one way of representing an organization is an organization chart (Figure 8.4). The model draws attention to such aspects of the organization as the division of tasks and responsibilities, reporting structures, spans of control, the formal power structure and lines of formal communication.

Another model of an organization (Figure 8.5) is the simple open-systems model. This model stimulates questions about suppliers, raw materials, financial resources, market conditions, products, monitoring systems, quality control, internal systems and procedures.

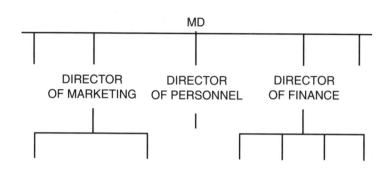

Figure 8.4   **Organization chart**

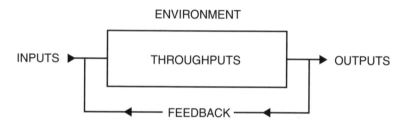

Figure 8.5   **Open-systems model**

The organization chart model is static, emphasizing structure; the systems model is dynamic, emphasizing exchange and process. Both are 'true', both are valuable and both are partial. As with the Gestalt psychologists'[6] experiments with perception we can only construe the world one way at a time. In the well-known example shown in Figure 8.6 at any moment we can *either* see a vase *or* see two faces in profile, but not both together.

Figure 8.6   **Vase or faces?**

From what has already been said it is clear that models can be as great a liability as they are an asset. Consultants with favourite models will gain a reputation for doing certain kinds of work because they will always construe organizational issues in the same way. Many external consultants have built successful businesses by marketing the approaches that flow from particular models – clients know in advance what they are likely to become involved in when they invite in certain consultants. Whether internal or external consultants, it seems to us particularly important not to become attached to a limited range of models that become a biased way of seeing.

There are other possible dangers in modelling:

- Over-simplification or over-generalization that leads to an elegant model but a distorted diagnosis.
- Over-elaboration, an attempt to account for everything in a model, so that clarity is lost.
- Trying to force fit a situation to a model and ignoring important incongruities.
- Allowing the model to become an end in itself, so that discussion of its validity becomes an avoidance of dealing with the actual situation.
- Over-emphasizing the objectivity of models and failing to recognize the assumptions, beliefs and values implicitly incorporated in them.

We hope that what we have said so far gives some idea of the enabling and paradoxically constraining nature of models.

Becoming conscious of models in use

Anyone working in the field of human resource development will already have a whole range of theories and rationales underpinning their work. These may cover leadership, conflict, group development, motivation, learning, communication, teamwork, management, change, selection, assessment and so on. The next stage of the consultant's development is recognizing how these ideas are providing models which inform his or her current practice.

When asked 'What model (of a group, an effective team, a successful planning process) were you using in designing this development activity?', it is surprising how many trainers we have worked with will look blank and reply 'I do not know that I was using any model'. The key words are 'I do not know'. If the design is not random, then behind it will be some kind of model, even if the trainer is unconscious of this. Further probing and 'unpacking' of the consultant's approach will invariably elicit the underlying models.

Initially people often need help in this kind of self-questioning. Although at first they may feel under test to 'prove' what they know, with genuine interest and encouragement most people's self-confidence blossoms as they engage in a process which helps them to realize how much they have already internalized. They become more rigorous and purposeful and more aware of the relation between their own framing of a situation and the work they do.

We talked with one internal consultant about a team-building event she was designing. Initially she declared that the design was based on R.M. Belbin's[7] research into team roles (Belbin suggested that people adopt one or more preferred roles in a team from a possible range of eight, each of which provides a valuable contribution to the team's ability to perform its tasks), but in further discussions with her it became clear that she was drawing on a number of other models without being fully aware of it:

- In considering who should be included in the team-building event, and also the extent to which internal relationships should be emphasized rather than the organizational context, she was drawing on her knowledge of *boundaries*.[8]
- In making decisions on how to manage the risk level she had a model of *group development*[9] in mind.
- In designing the flow of exercises and reviews she was influenced by *Kolb's learning cycle*.[10]

By bringing the underlying models to the surface she could immediately see where her design could be improved. It became clear to her where certain sequences of sessions were inappropriate and where she could meet several objectives simultaneously.

Experimenting with familiar models

We have seen many trainers paralyse themselves when faced with organizational work because they have rushed to an OD textbook in search of a method for organizational analysis, and then tried to apply approaches which they only partially understand. Although the models they have relied on to date will not be sufficient for organization change consulting, they provide a valuable starting point and they are at least imbued with the richness of real experience.

For example, a purely intrapersonal model may be useful for assessing aspects of organizational 'personality' or culture. Interpersonal models can help to diagnose interdepartmental issues. Developmental or life-stage models can illuminate the 'maturity' of an organization and its readiness for change. Models of adult learning can throw light on the idea of learning organizations. Frameworks for understanding the role of the individual counsellor can throw light on the relationship of consultant to total client system.

We now give some examples of the initial thoughts of trainers when asked to describe aspects of their organization using familiar models that they would usually apply to individuals or training groups. In each case some pointers towards diagnosis and action emerged, and it was clear that these increased the trainers' confidence in their ability to begin working at an organizational level.

Example 1: the Johari Window[11]

The model (Figure 8.7) was originally conceived to describe the self in interaction with others. The model suggests that self-disclosure to others and feedback from others considerably increases the area of effective 'free' activity and also slowly uncovers the unconscious potential of the individual.

This model was used by a training consultant to clarify his

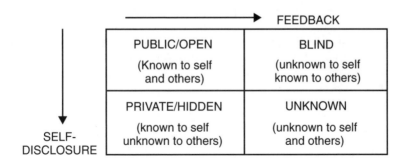

Figure 8.7   Johari Window

perceptions of the climate in a client company prior to reorganization of the field service operation. His task was to design courses to educate and train staff for their new roles and responsibilities. His data came from interviews with key personnel, both those instigating the change strategy and those affected by it.

He adapted the Johari Window as shown in Figure 8.8. He sorted the information and perceptions he had accumulated into the model. In general terms it then looked as it does in Figure 8.9.

	PUBLIC	BLIND
	Openly acknowledged. Clear to me and the organization.	Perceived by me, but the organizational members seem unaware.
	HIDDEN	UNKNOWN
	Privately acknowledged to me, but not made public.	Unclear to me or the organization.

ORGANIZATIONAL AWARENESS →

ORGANIZATIONAL DISCLOSURE ↓

Figure 8.8

PUBLIC/OPEN	BLIND
Published information and policy statements about the reasons for reorganization, the benefits of the proposed new structures. Existence of large numbers of rumours acknowledged. Some new appointments made.	To aspects of current culture that are inimical to the changes. To commonality of unvoiced concerns. To incompleteness of formal communications about changes. To paralysing effect of sense of powerlessness in parts of the organization.
PRIVATE/HIDDEN	UNKNOWN
Individual anxiety about career prospects. No discussion of the consequences of changes. Lack of certainty amongst decision-making management of final shape of changes. Criticism and suggestion not expressed upwards, only to peers.	Capacity to discover and devise new ways of working which release energy and motivation.

Figure 8.9

As he was encouraged to think in terms of a longer-term intervention strategy rather than a series of training courses, this consultant identified some options for proposals he could discuss with his clients:

1   Offer to work with the management team to help them clarify remaining uncertainties about the change strategy and to design a more effective communication process.
2   Suggest third-party facilitation of a consultative meeting between members of the management team and field staff to hear responses to and suggestions for improving the change plans.
3   Design a series of change implementation workshops attended by vertical slices of the organization instead of horizontal slices attending training courses as originally planned; devise a problem-solving approach where groups identify and work on some of the perceived blocks to the successful implementation of the changes.

Example 2: transactional analysis (TA)[12]
One of the fundamentals in TA is the analysis of individual functioning in terms of three ego states (parent, adult and child), each of which describes a coherent pattern of thoughts, feelings and behaviours. The model represents an individual as in Figure 8.10.

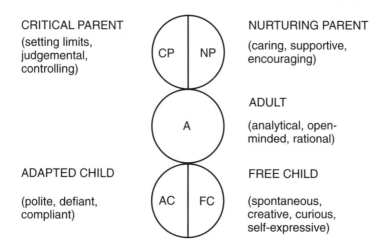

CRITICAL PARENT

(setting limits, judgemental, controlling)

CP   NP

NURTURING PARENT

(caring, supportive, encouraging)

A

ADULT

(analytical, open-minded, rational)

ADAPTED CHILD

(polite, defiant, compliant)

AC   FC

FREE CHILD

(spontaneous, creative, curious, self-expressive)

Figure 8.10   TA model

The model suggests that it is possible to construct ego-grams to represent the relative use of different ego states by an individual and to analyse characteristic ways in which each type of ego state is manifested.

A trainer used this idea to describe her organization, an insurance company. She then considered what new insight this gave her into the reasons why two interventions currently being implemented by the T & D department were meeting with very different degrees of success. (See Figure 8.11.)

The two interventions were both attempts to change the management style of the company in the light of new conditions in the financial market place. The company recognized the need to move from a bureaucratic to a more flexible, initiative-taking, customer-orientated culture.

One method was to provide interpersonal skills training

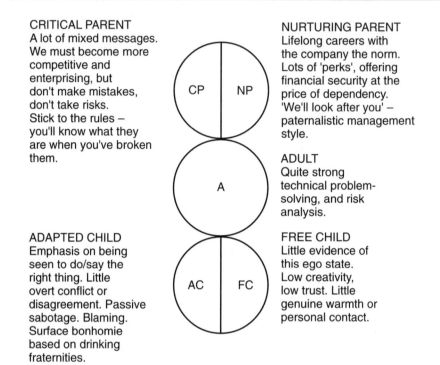

CRITICAL PARENT
A lot of mixed messages.
We must become more
competitive and
enterprising, but
don't make mistakes,
don't take risks.
Stick to the rules –
you'll know what they
are when you've broken
them.

NURTURING PARENT
Lifelong careers with
the company the norm.
Lots of 'perks', offering
financial security at the
price of dependency.
'We'll look after you' –
paternalistic management
style.

ADULT
Quite strong
technical problem-
solving, and risk
analysis.

ADAPTED CHILD
Emphasis on being
seen to do/say the
right thing. Little
overt conflict or
disagreement. Passive
sabotage. Blaming.
Surface bonhomie
based on drinking
fraternities.

FREE CHILD
Little evidence of
this ego state.
Low creativity,
low trust. Little
genuine warmth or
personal contact.

Figure 8.11

courses for the middle management layers in the company,
with an emphasis on building more open working relationships.
These programmes were foundering in a morass of anger, sus-
picion and fear. Despite careful pre-course briefing, during
which potential participants appeared willing and interested in
attending (saying the right thing), those leading the programmes were repeatedly faced with passively hostile groups
unwilling to work with the material.

From her analysis the trainer could see clearly that the courses
were aimed at activating the free child ego states, the least
robust and supported aspect of the company's 'personality'.
There had been no attempt to address the negative effects of
the parental messages. The programme rationale, which might
have been expected to appeal to the adult ego states, was based
on humanistic, self-awareness concepts, which were basically

alien to the culture. In all, the course fed directly into and actually reinforced the adapted child it was attempting to change.

A second initiative, based on analytical problem-solving and innovative teamwork, was much more successful. This built on the adult ego state by engaging managers in joint problem-solving on real business issues, using structured techniques. The difficult critical parent and adapted child areas were bypassed, while the free child was gently opened up by introducing cross-functional working, emphasizing joint problems rather than personalities and encouraging acceptance and curiosity in one another's ideas and potential contributions.

Example 3: Kolb's learning cycle

David Kolb's model of the learning process (Figure 8.12) identifies four essential activities. He also suggests that individuals will have preferred learning styles and particular difficulties.

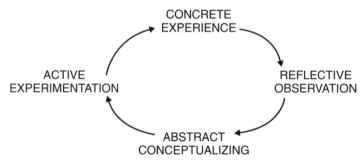

Figure 8.12   Kolb's learning cycle

Ben Bennett and Jim Richardson[13] applied this model to organizations to show how different kinds of culture or structure could inhibit different aspects of the learning cycle. (See Figure 8.13.)

In discussions with organizations on the design of a change strategy, which inevitably means learning new ways of working, this model aids diagnosis of the kind of activities the organization most needs to engage in, because they are the ones most

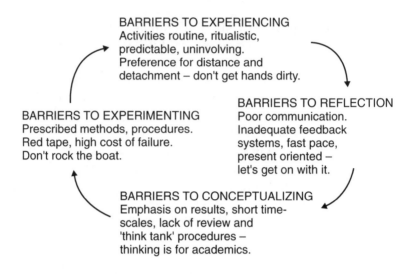

BARRIERS TO EXPERIENCING
Activities routine, ritualistic,
predictable, uninvolving.
Preference for distance and
detachment – don't get hands dirty.

BARRIERS TO REFLECTION
Poor communication.
Inadequate feedback
systems, fast pace,
present oriented –
let's get on with it.

BARRIERS TO EXPERIMENTING
Prescribed methods, procedures.
Red tape, high cost of failure.
Don't rock the boat.

BARRIERS TO CONCEPTUALIZING
Emphasis on results, short timescales, lack of review and
'think tank' procedures –
thinking is for academics.

Figure 8.13   Barriers to learning

likely to be avoided at present. The principle is to design interventions that will engage the organization members in the less
familiar learning styles as well as those which fit the structure
and culture of the company. For example, some organizations
can spend too much time reflecting and conceptualizing,
through the over-use of committees and by constant reference
of decisions up the hierarchy. They may need to be encouraged
to experiment with pilot projects.

Learning about a wider range of organizational models

This step involves familiarization with models designed
specifically to deal with organizational systems rather than individuals or groups. In fact trainers are often well acquainted
with some of these in the sense that they introduce managers to
them on courses; the development involves trainers in actually
applying them to organizational issues. An example might be
Kurt Lewin's force field analysis.[14] (See Figure 8.14.)

This model represents any situation as a dynamic equilibrium
between opposing forces. By analysing the range and strength
of forces acting in the *status quo*, trainers may discover possibilities for action in terms of:

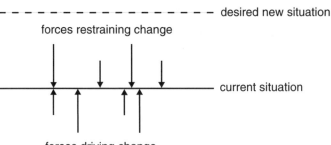

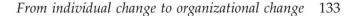

Figure 8.14   Force field analysis

- Introducing new driving forces.
- Reducing or redirecting restraining forces.
- Increasing driving forces (without creating an equal and opposite increase in restraining forces).

Although trainers are often familiar with this model as a problem-solving tool, they may be less aware of its value in mapping organizational dynamics in relation to a change goal.

Many other models for organizational diagnosis are derived from systems theory. They invite analysis in terms of the relationships between organizational inputs, outputs, through-puts, environment and feedback/monitoring systems. One such example is the model developed by Graham Pratt and Bob Lees (Figure 8.15). They use it in collaboration with their clients to arrive at a joint diagnosis. Below are some of the questions they might pose:

1 *Purpose.* What is the basic reason for the existence of the organization? Are people satisfied with this purpose? Is it related to environmental needs?
2 *Organizational strategy.* What is the general direction which the organization will pursue in order to achieve its purpose?
3 *Structure.* What is the relationship of the various functions to each other in the whole organization? Are there too many levels for effective communication? Are people comfortable

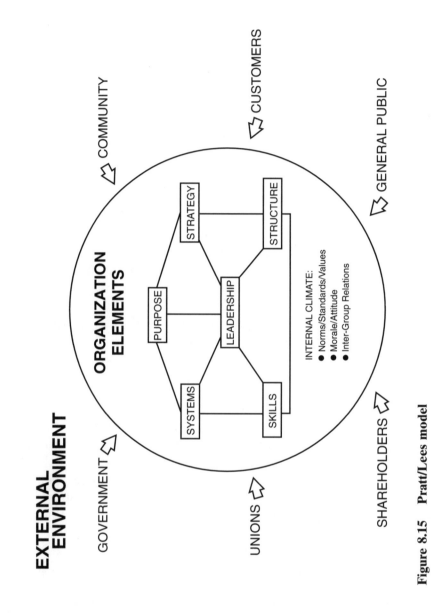

Figure 8.15 Pratt/Lees model

134

with today's structure? Should it be changed to support a new strategy and purpose? Are there some new roles that need to be developed?

4 *Systems.* Are regularly interacting and interdependent groups of activities forming a united whole? (Examples are work flow, job design, information flow, decision-making systems, committees/meetings, technology.)

5 *Skills.* What is the ability of individuals or work units to use knowledge and experience effectively in performing tasks or making decisions? Is there the necessary mix of managerial and technical skills to meet the challenge of the future? If the organization is changing, are any new skills needed?

6 *Internal climate.* What are the norms of generalized or collective behaviour in the organization? Are they changing? Do they need to change? What is valued, believed in by the members of the organization? As change takes place are there any values which need to be protected? If so, how? How effective are the relations between the different teams, divisions and departments in the organization?

7 *Leadership.* Do the leaders have a long-term vision for the organization? What types of leadership would support the organization's efforts to adjust to change?

8 *External environment.* Who are the outside parties that significantly affect the way the organization does its business? Does anything need to be done to improve relationships with any of these groups?

Other types of models fall into one or another of Gareth Morgan's[15] classification of organizational metaphors:

- Organizations as machines focusing on efficiency and rationality.
- Organizations as cultures focusing on history, rituals, beliefs and norms.
- Organizations as political systems focusing on power, competition and vested interests.
- Organizations as psyches focusing on patterns of unconscious processes.

- Organizations as organisms focusing on interdependence, growth and development.
- Organizations as brains focusing on creativity, information-processing and problem-solving.
- Organizations as flux and transformation focusing on change processes.

Sometimes trainers feel overwhelmed at the complexity of some of these metaphors, mistakenly believing that, in order to use them, they need to know about all aspects of a company. In fact the value of such metaphors to organization change consultants is in helping them formulate pertinent questions about the organization's functioning. The answers lie with their clients, and the model becomes an aid to joint understanding and intervention design.

Creating one's own models

Once consultants stop being overawed by models, they become increasingly able to 'play' with them as liberating and effective tools for gaining fresh insights into organizational issues. Some models may be creative and metaphorical, e.g. representing interdepartmental relationships as an extended family. These 'models' emerge simply from a willingness to be uninhibited and to say 'This state of affairs is just like . . .' Very often in fitting aspects of the actual situation to the metaphor, the trainer finds that the model breaks down, but its usefulness lies in the discussion it generates and the possible interrelationships of cause and effect it suggests.

For example, one rich analogy is to liken the organization to a sport. This approach recently generated a lot of fun and insights with a group of managers who saw their company like a game of football. The problem as they saw it was that:

- The coach kept running on to the pitch and started playing.
- Extra footballs were randomly thrown onto the pitch.
- In the middle of the game players were suddenly told to play for the other side (without changing their strips).

Working with this analogy they were able to identify some options (e.g. distract the coach with other problems) and translate these back into their work. One of the managers arranged to share regular and frequent briefing sessions with the 'coach' in order to keep him off the field of play.

Other models are created by the more painstaking process of arranging and rearranging information about a situation, grouping certain aspects, ordering, classifying and symbolizing until a coherent framework begins to emerge. The analysis becomes a useful model once the representation of the situation becomes recognizable to others in the organization and invites discussion and hypothesis.

Clarity of purpose

We have suggested that consultants need to develop ways of thinking about organizations, through the use of conceptual models. Taking the view that all action by consultants in a client system is an intervention means that clarity of purpose is vital, if consultants are not to become hopelessly entangled in the complexities of the system they are working with. Organization models provide one way of keeping sight of the wood when deep among the trees. Other ways of thinking about this complexity are introduced in Chapter 11.

Clarity of purpose is also based on awareness of one's own aims and beliefs, which comes from knowing the answers to such questions as:

- 'What sort of organizations do I want to help create?'
- 'What sort of work do I really want to do?'
- 'What sort of relationships do I want to build with my clients?'
- 'What values underpin my work?'
- 'How will I handle organizational politics?'
- 'Are there certain assignments I will refuse?'
- 'How will I resolve questions of confidentiality?'

Consultants with some clarity about their own assumptions and intentions are likely to be better equipped to help clients recognize and clarify the way they are thinking about the direction of their organization.

Notes

1   Beckhard, R. *Organization Development: Strategies and Models*, Addison-Wesley 1969.
2   McLean, A.J., Sims, D.B.P., Maugham, I.L., Tuffield, . *Organization Development in Transition – Evidence of an Evolving Profession*, Wiley 1982.
3   Tannenbaum, R. (ed.) *Human Systems Development*, Jossey-Bass 1985.
4   Lippitt, G.L. *Visualizing Change: Model Building and the Change Process*, University Associates 1973.
5   Lippitt, ibid.
6   Kohler, W. *Gestalt Psychology*, New American Library 1975.
7   Belbin, R.M. *Management Teams: Why They Succeed or Fail*, Heinemann 1981.
8   Phillips, K. 'Boundaries and Boundary Management in Interpersonal Skills Training', *Journal of European Industrial Training*, Vol. 7, No. 3, 1983.
9   Porter, L. and Mohr (eds) *Reading Book for Human Relations Training*, N.T.L. Institute 1982.
10   Kolb, D.A., Rubin, I.M. and McIntyre, J.M. *Organizational Psychology – An Experiential Approach*, Prentice-Hall 1974.
11   Porter and Mohr, op. cit.
12   Barker, D. *TA and Training*, Gower 1980.
13   Bennett, B. and Richardson, J., 'Applying Learning Techniques to On-the-job Development', *Journal of European Industrial Training'*, Vol. 8, No. 1, 1984.
14   Lewin, K. *Field Theory in Social Science*, Harper and Row 1951.
15   Morgan, G. *Images of Organization*, Sage 1997.

9 The organization change consultant

This chapter describes in more detail the consulting project, extending over one year, outlined briefly in Chapter 2. It is chosen to illustrate how an initial request for training courses had the potential for an organization change intervention. Although we undertook the project as external consultants, it is likely to be similar in its starting point to the situation facing many trainers and developers moving into internal consulting roles. Often their potential clients will still expect them to provide training courses for individuals, but if their own perspective is that of organizational change, they will be able to widen the scope of their work.

An organization change assignment

Initial contact

We received a telephone call from Adrian Croft, the Head of Training of Bolton-Smith Ltd. He had heard that we ran training courses for trainers becoming consultants; he wanted us to run a similar programme, suitably modified, for IT specialists. We said that the modifications could well be extensive, since the range of skills that trainers would bring to such a programme were likely to be very different from those of computer specialists. That said, we agreed to meet in order to discuss possibilities.

In preparing for the meeting we decided to resist pressure simply to run an in-house version of the open course. We wanted to learn a lot more about the context in which the need for this training had been identified.

When we got to the meeting there were two others present apart from Adrian Croft. These were Geoff Keen, the Personnel Manager, and John Williams, Director of the Information Technology Division.

Essentially the need for consultancy skills training arose out of Bolton-Smith's long-established tradition of working as expert technical consultants. They were now discovering the need to work more collaboratively with their clients, and appreciated that such collaboration was one of the most effective ways of securing follow-up work. At present they had too many one-off assignments and their status in the market place was generally 'second division'; they were having difficulty securing assignments in the management consultancy field which they saw as an expanding market.

The IT Division had been identified as the prime target for training, which would then be extended to other divisions, including financial and economic planning and market studies.

In probing for the broader context within which the training was wanted, we learned that the whole strategy for the company was under review. There was, in particular, a debate about whether to:

- Decentralize and set up regional centres.
- Break down the existing divisions and regroup them according to market sectors.
- Set up a separate management consultancy group.

Although the legitimacy of our questions about these broader issues was recognized, our clients still saw us very much as training consultants. We spent some time discussing our role with them, pointing out in particular that the manner in which we worked needed to mirror the aims of the assignment. It was a glaring contradiction for us to operate as prescriptive experts when this was exactly the style of consultancy they wanted to move away from. We explained that in experimenting together with a more collaborative approach we and they would learn a great deal more about the organization's potential difficulties in changing their own consultancy style.

Looking back on the meeting, we realized this was the most critical part of it. Our clients accepted the validity of what we were saying at a cognitive level, but felt anxious about engaging with us in a mode they were unsure how to manage. The greater ambiguity inherent in the consultancy style that they wanted to develop and which they were experiencing with us gave them cause for thought.

The meeting closed with a discussion about fees and our agreement to write a formal proposal. We were told that Geoff Keen would be our client contact for the day-to-day management of the project and he would liaise closely with John Williams; Adrian Croft would be responsible for ultimately guiding the extension of the assignment to the other divisions.

Initial proposal

CONSULTANT DEVELOPMENT IN THE IT DIVISION OF BOLTON-SMITH LTD

PRESENTING SITUATION – the need for change.
Bolton-Smith offers services which cover both traditional consultancy and newer areas of activity such as information technology.

Historically, the 'prescriptive' mode of consultation has been used and indeed expected by your clients. You have identified the need for a more flexible collaborative consultancy style to meet the emerging demands of the market place, especially in providing an integrated management consultancy service.

THE FOCUS FOR CHANGE – target population.

At present the need for change is perceived most clearly in the Information Technology Division. John Williams, the divisional director, sees this as an urgent operational requirement in the face of the following situation:

(a)   The division is expanding rapidly with an expected intake of 120 people over the next 3 years.

(b)   About one-third of this intake is likely to come from the software houses or new graduates. These recruits are likely to be highly competent within their technical specialism but will have more limited knowledge, skills and experience of consulting.

(c)   Because of the historical situation indicated above, both new recruits with some consulting experience and existing Bolton-Smith staff are likely to be more familiar with a 'prescriptive' consulting style than any other.

Discussions between John Williams, Geoff Keen (Personnel Manager) and Adrian Croft (Director of Training and Recruitment) have resulted in a decision to resource a comprehensive training and development strategy to enhance the consulting skills of the IT Division.

DESIRED OUTCOMES

We believe that some further work is needed to specify these more precisely, but from our discussions so far we identified the following changes as being characteristic of the outcomes you are looking for:

1   *A change in attitude*: the staff in the IT Division to see themselves as *consultants* rather than IT specialists. This implies that they understand the nature of the consulting process and recognize that their competence in managing this process is as vital to their effectiveness as their technical knowledge and expertise.

2   *An increase in the level of consulting skill*: consultants to be able to intervene effectively at each stage of the consulting process and to be able to identify and adopt the consultancy style most suitable for different clients and different situations.

3   *A shorter induction period*: new consultants to become fully effective more quickly.
4   *Improved consulting teamwork*: consultants brought together for a particular project to establish effective working teams on the basis of a shared understanding of the aims and methods of consulting in Bolton-Smith.
5   *A reduction in the level of disaffection currently identified among some IT consultants*: consultants to feel well trained, prepared and supported by Bolton-Smith for the consulting projects they are asked to undertake.
6   *Greater retention of 'able' staff*: consultants to believe that Bolton-Smith offers opportunities for professional development that are not matched by rival firms. This implies that training in consulting skills is part of a wider career development strategy.

We enclose the outlines of two options for addressing these needs. The first represents what we see as the minimum commitment to mount a pilot training event, followed by a series of training courses. The second option sees consulting skills training as part of a wider change intervention. Clearly, there are a number of other possibilities which would combine elements from both options.

OPTION 1
Training to meet the immediate need

1   Identification of training needs by:
    (a)   Further discussions with Geoff Keen and John Williams.
    (b)   Interviews with some IT consultants, including both those with considerable experience and those relatively new to the division.

At this stage we would be able to judge whether the training needs could all be met within a single mixed-ability training event. Alternatively the needs might be sufficiently diverse to require two distinct modules: the first, an introduction to consultancy skills for new entrants, the second an advanced programme for more experienced consultants.

2   Establishing specific training objectives.

3   Designing, running and evaluating a pilot training event. The course design and content will be based on aspects of the consultancy cycle as described below:

Stages in consultancy	*Related issues*
1 Gaining entry.	How to establish credibility (dealing with early impressions, past reputations and stereotyped assumptions).
2 Building a working relationship and contracting.	How to clarify mutual expectations and responsibilities.
3 Clarifying purpose and desired outcomes.	How to test and develop commitment.
4 Data collection and diagnosis.	How to deal with issues of trust, conflict, anxiety, status, etc.
5 Designing strategies and plans for achieving desired outcomes.	How to engage in joint problem-solving. How to identify and harness organizational resources.
6 Monitoring implementation and identifying possible follow-up.	How to avoid mutual dependency.
7 Disengagement.	How to obtain closure.

4   Estimate of the time required

(a)   Identifying training needs   – 3 consultant days

(b)   Establishing objectives, designing course and materials   – 5 consultant days

(c)   Leading programme   – 4 consultant days

(d)   Evaluation and follow-up   – 2 consultant days

5   Implications

Benefits

(a)   This option could be put into effect quite quickly to meet the urgent current need.

(b)   Data which can be used for further honing of a full
      training and development strategy will be generated.
(c)   A modular approach (foundation training + follow-
      up) would provide professional development for IT
      consultants.

Concerns

(a)   Course learning may not be fully transferred to
      consultants' work if there is no general awareness
      of, and commitment to, the need for a change in
      consultancy style within the division allied to new
      business goals.
(b)   The training may be seen as divorced from and
      unsupported by management practices regarding
      recruitment, appraisal, career development,
      administrative systems, marketing strategy and so on.

The second option describes a broader approach to the assignment
which takes account of these concerns.

OPTION 2
Changing the consultancy style in the IT Division

1   Overview. See Figure 9.1.
2   Estimate of the time required. It is difficult at this stage to
    estimate the total time needed for the project. We would need
    to clarify the boundaries of each segment, the nature of our
    involvement and agree consultant time for each one. For
    example, the first stage might involve us facilitating a 1- or 2-
    day meeting of the management team to crystallize the kind of
    management consultancy service Bolton-Smith wants to be able
    to offer. With preliminary work this would mean 3 or 4
    consultant days.
3   Implications. From our discussions with you, we know that you
    are already thinking about the change process along these lines.
    Our reason for seeing this as a separate option is that here the
    consulting skills training forms part of the overall development
    strategy *from the outset*, whereas in Option 1, it may well form a
    first step towards it. The two options have different implications
    for the nature of our working relationship and mutual
    expectations.

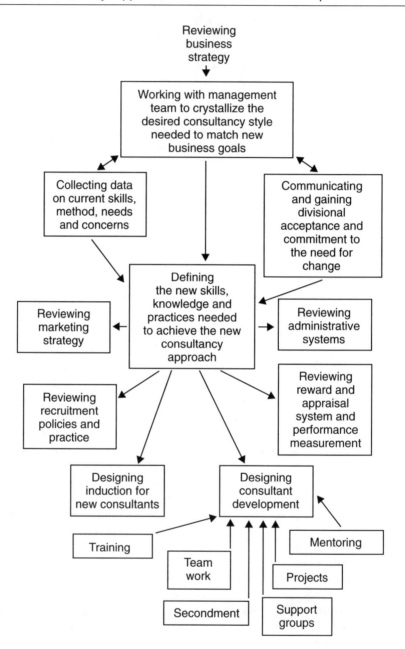

Figure 9.1

4 Fees. For either option our fees would be £⎯⎯⎯ per consultant day + expenses + VAT.

Commentary on the proposals

1 They emphasize the organizational context within which the training is intended to take place.
2 They concentrate on outcomes rather than means, thereby allowing scope for extensive collaboration with the client in the design and management of the project.
3 We offered both a training consultancy and an organization change consultancy option, giving the client a sense of the possible scope of the project while also offering some limited first steps (a pilot training programme or a management strategy meeting) where our relationship could be tested before further commitment was made.

There was a month's delay before we received a formal response to our proposals. A follow-up call with Geoff Keen revealed that further discussions with more senior management were taking place. Eventually we were invited to take part in an exploration of 'options somewhere between 1 and 2 as outlined in your proposal'. This involved:

- Meeting the Managing Director to discuss how our proposals fitted into plans for creating a new management consulting group.
- Extending the project to cover all divisions that would form part of this new group.
- Undertaking data collection interviews with a selection of consultants from all the divisions, some new to Bolton-Smith, others experienced consultants. Geoff Keen organized the interview schedule and briefed participants about the background.
- Scheduling a feedback meeting with the MD and divisional directors at which further plans would be discussed.

Data collection and diagnosis

In our interviews with the consultants we were seeking information about:

1   Consultancy as it was actually practised in Bolton-Smith.
2   In what way, if at all, management consultancy was seen as different from technical consulting.
3   How prepared and able consultants felt to undertake management consultancy.
4   The extent to which consultants felt supported in their work with clients by the organizational structure and practices of Bolton-Smith.
5   How much awareness there was of the changes being discussed at senior levels.
6   The consultants' own perceptions of the need for change in Bolton-Smith.

Bearing in mind that we were acting as consultants to consultants, we also asked each person, towards the end of the interview, for comments on our approach and how it was similar or different from the way in which they might have handled the interviews themselves. What was most interesting about this was that no one we spoke to had drawn a parallel between our work with Bolton-Smith as an organization and their own work with clients. It was clear that they saw themselves as problem-solvers not change agents.

The interview data provided some insight into the internal climate:

- Little liaison between divisions, manifested by unwillingness to share information or pass on work, and by ignorance and discounting of each other's activities.
- High value placed on individual autonomy and responsibility. Attempts at teamwork unsatisfactory because of individual competitiveness. Issues arising in teams inadequately addressed. Lack of team membership and leadership skills perceived.

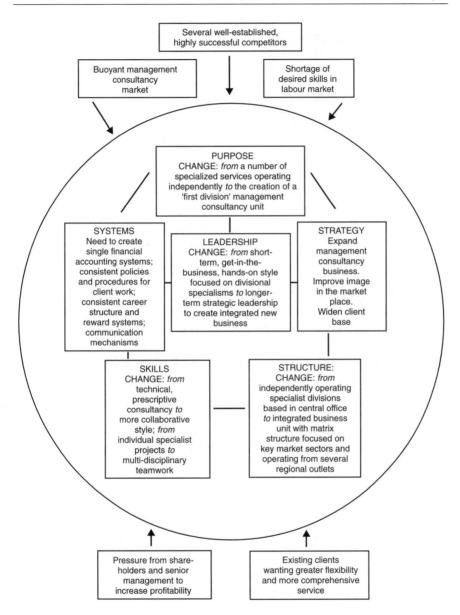

Figure 9.2   Application of Pratt/Lees model

- Senior managers out and about a lot with clients, devoting little time to internal management.
- Individuals identify with high professional standards in their field, but have little sense of what it means to be a Bolton-Smith consultant. Lack of shared purpose and values or identification with company.
- No common understanding of the nature of management consultancy.
- No targeting for type and quality of assignments. Getting in business of any kind is the priority.

With the data generated so far we put together a summary of the situation as we saw it, using the Pratt/Lees model described in Chapter 8. (See figure 9.2.)

Feedback meeting with clients

At this meeting with the MD and divisional directors we presented the data and invited responses and discussion. The reaction to this was very positive, even though we were simply presenting to the directors what had been said to us. It was clear that in so doing we were making explicit things which had never been fully articulated or openly discussed, and so had remained apparently unmanageable.

The directors, like their own consultants, were far more comfortable dealing with technical matters related to their specialisms than with issues related to the culture and climate of the company. Indeed they did not really have a language for doing this. It was also clear that there was a big communication gap between the senior management group and the consulting staff. The former did little to elicit information or response from staff, although they were very interested in the data we presented. Their notion of management communication was one way, top-down, and limited to the occasional circulation of written memoranda.

From the discussion we logged agreement on the following points:

1   It would be impossible to divorce the development of con-

sulting skills from the wider issues of change in the company. The move to management consultancy represented a drastic revision of the aims and nature of consulting work as currently practised. Although skill development was necessary for increasing consultant confidence in the non-technical aspects of their work, it would not suffice in creating the new kind of consultancy the directors wanted.

2 The lack of emphasis on collaborative work with clients was mirrored by lack of collaboration within the company. Both needed to be addressed simultaneously so that there was a consistency of working practice internally and externally. The proposed multi-disciplinary team approach would founder without this.

3 Full and visible direction and support would be needed from the management team in leading the change.

4 Involvement of consultant staff in the planning process would gain commitment to and identification with the new business group.

Design work

The next stage of the contract was to design a development strategy in collaboration with Geoff Keen. Instead of running a training course in consultancy skills, the plan was to bring together a group of consultants who had the potential to create and carry forward a change programme. Geoff Keen had the task of selecting key people from all the divisions who were sources of influence because of their experience, position, ability or personality. We undertook to prepare an outline design proposal for a residential workshop.

At our next meeting with Geoff Keen, pursuing the collaborative approach, we arrived with our design proposals on large pieces of flipchart paper with options and areas of uncertainty clearly visible. Although a little surprised at first, since his own model of expert consultancy inclined him to expect us to arrive with a polished formal proposal, he was soon involved with us, marker in hand, amending and building on our design ideas.

By the end of the meeting he was enthusiastic and had a sense of ownership of the design. He was keen to present it to the directors as a joint proposal. He had undertaken to research and prepare certain aspects of the workshop and was willing to take a leading role during it.

We discussed with him the assignment's progress and he began to talk about what he had noticed about our approach, comparing it with the more prescriptive style common in Bolton-Smith. He agreed that he would be willing to discuss these perceptions openly on the workshop.

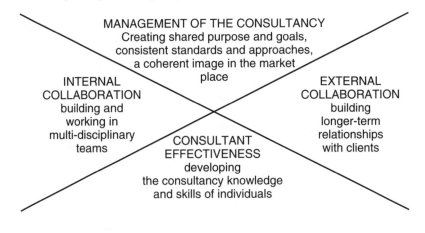

Figure 9.3

The workshop design addressed four areas, as shown in Figure 9.3. The key features of the design were:

1   The workshop was to be opened by the Managing Director giving the background to the project, outlining the plans for the management consultancy group, identifying areas of uncertainty and inviting the group to influence the future direction of the business. This would be done through the presentation of ideas and proposals at a meeting with the senior management team on the last day.
2   Various models of consultancy and consulting purposes would be introduced to the group; with these in mind, representatives from each of the divisions would discuss their current work and make presentations. Plenary sessions

would examine the differences and the common ground between divisions.

3 Mixed divisional groups would be formed to meet regularly during the week. Their task would be to:
   - Learn about interdisciplinary teamwork.
   - Support their members in a stocktake of skills and the identification of areas for development.
   - Identify the desired characteristics of management consultancy in Bolton-Smith.
   - Work with self-generated and specially prepared case studies so that a common approach could be created for dealing with some of the more typical consulting assignments.

4 As the week progressed the most important issues would be identified and on the penultimate day these would be sifted for relevance in the following day's presentation to senior management. Close attention would be paid to how these ideas, together with recommendations, should be presented; essentially the participants would be acting as internal consultants to the senior management team.

Outcomes from the assignment

In general terms the most significant result of the project was the improvement in communication, both between the senior managers and the rest of the staff and between the divisions. The directors came to the last morning of the workshop somewhat apprehensive about the possibility of being blamed for the difficulties the consultants were experiencing in their work. The participants themselves feared that their suggestions would simply be swept aside. Since none of these fears were realized, trust grew and some foundations for change within the organization were laid.

Specifically the outcomes were:

- The initiation of cross-divisional meetings to talk about projects and identify areas for collaboration.
- The establishment of two project teams: one to write a draft document articulating the purpose, values and approaches

which would characterize consultancy in Bolton-Smith; the other to make proposals for standardized procedures and documentation, when working with clients.

- A presentation by a subset of the consultant group to the management team of the whole organization.
- A follow-up day with the participants to consider the progress so far and to identify further development needs. Three members of the group described in some detail a major success in working collaboratively with a new client.
- A decision to mount another workshop, two of whose features would be:
  - Considering how to direct the business into market sector groups.
  - Some representatives from the previous group would work with us for part of the workshop to pass on the progress made so far and to describe their own experiences in applying their learning.

Postscript

Six months after the events we have described the parent organization took the decision that the management consultancy operations were not viable within the aims of the company and the entire initiative came to a halt – thus underlining some of the points made in the previous chapter about organization change consultancy, in particular that the consultants' working boundaries need to be drawn as inclusively as possible. In this case we gave scant attention to the boundary between the management consultancy and the rest of the firm. Instead, we concentrated on the apparently successful changes taking place, ignoring the larger context and the forces within it which were not supportive of those changes.

We also allowed ourselves to be lulled into dropping our original proposal for initial work with the management consultancy's directors to clarify and strengthen their strategy. As we have illustrated here, working in the interstices of an organization to create change from the bottom up can be very effective; but in the end, if it is not accompanied by equivalent work from the top down, then new initiatives will always be vulnerable.

10 From training to consulting: the team dimension

Keri Phillips

The move from training to consulting often takes place within a team. A common scenario is an internal training group which, for reasons described elsewhere, then needs to work as consultants. Indeed such a move is often part of a repositioning by the whole of the Human Resources function. In this transition, or in many instances revolution, the divisive forces pulling the team apart increase just at a time when there is a need for greater cohesiveness. This is the first theme of this chapter. Much of what I describe below is concerned with the 'shadow side'[1,2] of organizations, namely a darker aspect of organizational life which is either not acknowledged or even recognized. My emphasis here is on the difficulties but I would not wish the reader to assume that these are inevitable. Teams can be sources of great joy and excitement; the move to consultancy an energizing new stage in professional and personal development. However, this is not always so, and my purpose is to explore the issues starkly. The second theme looks at the practical steps for building a high-quality professional consulting team, bearing in mind the potential difficulties.

157

The divisive forces

Many of the divisive forces are practical and logistical, but inevitably have an interwoven emotional dimension. I shall cover both aspects. Consultancy, in contrast with training, is often fragmented and unpredictable. Hence it is quite likely that a team of consultants will be out on the road, frequently as individuals, engaged in a wide variety of activities (e.g. initial client meeting, process facilitation, running a two-day change management workshop). Under these circumstances it is easy for colleagues to lose track of each other. This is likely to be in sharp contrast to earlier days when the training team might well have been running courses on their own premises and it would have been much easier to meet. Even if they were working separately in hotels the greater predictability of work-load would have made it easier to plan meetings. Against this backdrop the chances of misunderstandings and breakdowns in communication increase: 'Do I *really* know what Jane agreed with that client?' 'Is Joe making commitments that we do not have the resources to meet?' 'At what stage of development is each project?' 'Where *is* Bill?'

None of these practical and emotional problems is insurmountable; they do, however, require time and attention as the personal challenges are multiplied and magnified in a team setting. For some the move from training to consulting can be particularly demanding because it may mean, as described in Chapter 3, relinquishing or reducing strong needs for power, performing and predictability. For some, these needs may have been well established from childhood. When these needs are no longer, or not sufficiently, met then the consultant may respond in many ways, both conscious and unconscious:

- Seeking to create certainty where it does not and cannot exist.
- Reassessing the expectations of self and others.

- Negotiating and contracting a new set of relationships and ways of working.
- Imagining, and indeed superimposing, a view of others to justify personal needs.
- Looking for reassurance.
- Over-commitment in an attempt to make oneself indispensable.

It is simplistic to talk of these as healthy or unhealthy responses, because ultimately people are doing what they need to in trying to take care of themselves. Also we can be adept at appearing to handle a situation 'well' whilst in fact denying reality, e.g. be rewriting job descriptions whilst burying feelings of anger and fear. My purpose here is not to describe and analyse all the self-protective patterns which may take place. However, I would say that just when the team needs to be at its most clear thinking and clear feeling, it may be at its most confused, paradoxically bringing the worst out in each other, e.g. if everybody is longing for reassurance, who will actually give it? If none is given then the need for it is likely to increase; a vicious circle then follows. I shall now illustrate this further.

There are many theories for looking at patterns of behaviour and identifying where relationships may consequently get into difficulty. One of these, which I will outline and then link back to consultancy, is based upon the idea of abandonment and engulfment phobias.[3,4] Abandonment phobia is a fear of being left alone, totally deserted. Engulfment phobia is a fear of being overwhelmed, swamped by others. The underlying principle is that in times of stress and difficulty, some people will have a tendency toward abandonment phobia, others will move towards engulfment phobia. Such moves may be fleeting or a more regular feature of their lives. The prompts for these phobias may, to the casual observer, be very apparent or, to all intents and purposes, non-existent. So, a consultant might move into *abandonment* phobia because of:

- *No apparent reason.* The consultant looks as if he is working well and effectively, but has in fact become very weary, feeling isolated through spending so much time alone in hotels and training centres.

- *Minimal.* Being the last to receive their personal development discussion from their manager.
- *Moderate.* A recognition within the consulting team that there is not enough work to sustain existing staff numbers.
- *Strong.* Being told he is surplus to requirements.

A consultant might move into *engulfment* phobia because of:

- *No apparent reason.* The consultant is doing a good job but has become drained by encountering so many people and their problems. She longs for the time to recuperate.
- *Minimal.* Being given responsibility for developing a new and rather needy consultant.
- *Moderate.* At the end of a heavy schedule of work the consultant is asked to spend a week hosting a large group of overseas visitors.
- *Strong.* The consultant is under great pressure to give body and soul to work, including attending team barbecues at the weekend!

These sets of examples can only be very crude illustrations since, as is well known, one person's stress is another's delight and stimulation.

The underlying patterns of engulfment and abandonment phobias may well have been established within each individual for many years. When stimulated they may have an intensity and manifestation which is more appropriate to the past than the present, e.g. the minimal abandonment trigger mentioned above may lead to old fears (not being valued by my boss, teacher, father), which may or may not be evident for others to see. It may not be evident because survival and success in organizations is often at the cost of denying one's own feelings, i.e. it is not acceptable to appear scared or vulnerable, even though the realities of business life these days mean that such feelings are likely to occur. People then become skilled in presenting the appearance of 'being alright'. It is likely that the more skilled they are in this then the less likely their underlying needs (e.g. for support) will be recognized and met. Their anxiety consequently increases and they have to work harder at 'keeping up appearances'. All this can consume a lot of energy, energy which paradoxically is not available for moving the organization forward. The irony is that with today's great emphasis on quality, it is increasingly recognized that excellence can only come from the heart, i.e. a sincere desire to make continuous improvements. It is surely misguided and unrealistic to expect people only to bring to work that bit of their heart which is enthusiastic and motivated and not that which is uncertain and scared!

I now want to link this back to consultancy: the anxieties about moving from training to consulting may stimulate engulfment and abandonment phobias within the team. Those fearing abandonment may well want to get closer, either to each other (possibly creating a blinkered incestuousness) or to others, who in fact fear engulfment. The latter then retreat, being pursued by those who want to get closer . . . Each is fulfilling the other's worst fears. Each behaves in a way that ensures that ultimately they do not get what they want. Energy is spent proving points about the relationship and confirming assumptions (often archaic) rather than dealing with current practical realities.[5] Any or all of this might happen outside conscious awareness; it may be a pattern of behaviour which has become an ingrained habit. It is a path of least resistance which defines how the person sees particular aspects of the world; it becomes their truth. As a very rough guide, the earlier in life 'the truth' was acquired then the less easily the habits and beliefs attached to it are amenable to change. The simple presentation of incontrovertible information may be insufficient. A compulsive procrastinator may genuinely not believe they keep putting off decisions; particularly if the information is given to them by somebody they see as impetuous! The actions and reactions are then on automatic pilot rather than made through active choice.

So the worst case scenario is that the team is an emotional cauldron with lots of feelings which are scarcely recognized or understood either by self or others. At such a time the team may well be expected to be a source of clarity and sanity in the organization, spearheading and stoutly supporting change. The pressure to be something one is not can also create additional strains. The strain of maintaining a façade of being grown up and in control (like all good consultants should be!) whilst actually feeling confused, alone and rejected. Once again this is the possible source of another vicious circle: the consultant works hard to put on a professional appearance, smoothly working through an element of the consulting cycle (procedure), but denying (consciously or unconsciously) her own needs (process); the client consequently feels treated more as a number than a person and rejects the consultant's work, thus causing the consultant to feel even less valued. If the atmosphere in the consulting team is, or seems to be, unsupportive, then relationships with clients can become increasingly problematic. For example:

- A sympathetic, likeable and welcoming client is over-indulged.
- Unexpressed anger and frustration is redirected towards the client (anger can have many manifestations – not listening properly, not fulfilling commitments, subtle put-downs).
- An unwillingness by the consultant to close a project (abandonment phobia?).
- A greater emphasis on basing the consultancy on a series of ephemeral relationships with clients, who may anyway feed this inclination through their desire for quick fixes (engulfment phobia?).

In all this the need for understanding and engagement within the team is likely to be greater than it was in the past. Course participants can go through the motions. Clients are much less likely to, because careers and operational requirements are much more at stake. Good-quality contracting requires the consultant to work with some of the personal fears and aspirations of the client. That is the client's heart. A way of achieving this degree of humanity, understanding and skill is to work not just at the same level, *but a bit deeper*, with colleagues. The parallels with the work of a trainer are very clear.

Many training activities require participants to take some personal risk, i.e. to move beyond their comfort zone. The trainer intervenes to generate enough feeling of risk in the participants that they have energy to learn, but do not feel so much at risk that people are immobilized or defensive (see Figure 10.1). In order for the trainer to make some informed decisions about risk levels and their appropriateness she should have been a trainee in similar activities, and experienced them at a rather higher level of risk than she will be operating at as a trainer. This is not an option, but an ethical necessity. A similar obligation applies to the consultant. The consultant needs to have a pretty good understanding of her own needs, feelings and anxieties in order to work with clients who may have similar concerns and vulnerabilities. This is not a subtle invitation for the consultant to act as a therapist. Rather it is about having sufficient self-knowledge *not* to try and act as a therapist; to have a sufficiently rich repertoire to do what is necessary, e.g. noticing the client's unease, not feeling unbalanced by it and then exercising choices about whether to comment on it then, later, or not at all. This capability, which does not mean always knowing exactly what to do, is greatly enhanced if the

Figure 10.1

team uses such skills with each other, for example in self-development groups. Here they can be practised, discussed and used to support mutual learning.

The consulting team will therefore need to be of the highest quality to meet the range of challenges likely to arise. For example, the model in Figure 10.2 describes in broad terms the type of team-building assignments the consultants might be asked to carry out. The timescale axis is hopefully self-explanatory. The openness axis refers to the extent to which members of the team will need to be honest and straightforward about themselves and the task. The team-building need, as initially manifested, could be in any of the four domains; further data collection and analysis may, however, locate it elsewhere.

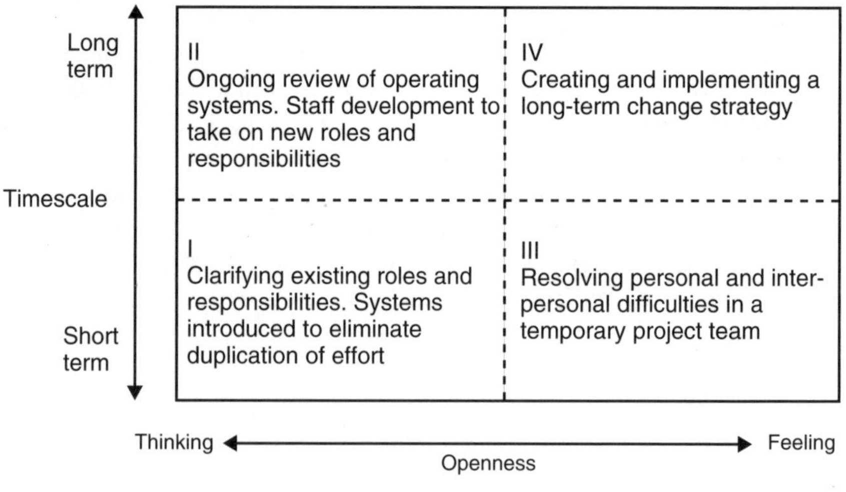

Figure 10.2   Domains of team-building

At first the need may be seen as one of identifying ways of improving existing working practices because of some immediate problems, e.g. duplication of effort, crucial information going missing (Box I in Figure 10.2). This may then lead in a number of directions:

• The establishment of longer-term plans for enhancing the

quality of working systems and planning staff development to support this (Box II in Figure 10.2).

- The realization that there are underlying relationships issues which may need to be dealt with. Namely, that feelings have to be explored before agreements about how working systems can be made (Box III in Figure 10.2).
- The recognition that a longer-term strategy for the group/ organization has to be in place. This necessitates people being very open about their personal ambitions and concerns (Box IV in Figure 10.2).

For a consulting team to move freely in working within and across all four domains it will need to have built itself as a team in all aspects covered by the model; without this it can have no legitimacy based on competence.

Building a high-quality consulting team

When organizations are in turbulence, often the case these days, then the consulting team needs to muster as much clarity as possible; otherwise it will either *export* its own confusion, consciously or unconsciously loading the client with even more problems, or *import* the organization's confusion and become incapacitated through information overload, trying to please too many people and absorbing anger and frustration. In other words the team needs to be skilled in boundary management: it is open to the organization but does not let itself get overwhelmed by it. The team has a sense of its own identity, without being élitist, being both apart from and a part of the organization. This is similar to how a trainer's relationship with a group is likely to be best managed. The team's personality is neither engulfment nor abandonment phobic. All this is about establishing a secure professional home base from which consultants can move out into the organization with sufficient confidence, and to which they can return being sure of a place where they can gain some respite, respect and challenge.

It is arguable that the boundary management skills need to

be of a far higher order, and are indeed of greater importance, for internal as opposed to external consulting teams. Internal consulting teams are quite often created in the organization's image, e.g. a perfectionist organization may well have a perfectionist internal consulting team. They can then seduce each other into ineffectiveness, in a relentless search for complete data which means that action is never taken. There are also the practical issues such as the request to 'pop along for a chat', which can mean that work has started and assumptions have been made without proper contracting. The initial boundaries are so blurred that teasing them apart is necessary for the work to begin. All this can be quite different from the external consulting team which is more obviously and consciously invited across the boundary of the organization. Where internal consultants can charge for their services, this can be a great aid to boundary clarification and management since the prospective client will need to consider, as with an external consultant, questions such as 'Can I afford them?' 'Do I really want them?' 'Can I justify this cost?'

However, another perspective on this is that if clients have been accustomed to receiving training and consultancy services without direct cost to themselves then the introduction of hard charging can alienate. Prospective clients may now find it difficult to see value in the internal consultant. 'If I have to pay, then I might as well see the full range of what is available both internally and externally.' In response, the internal consulting team may wish to seek out ways of stimulating business without at first charging clients.

Creating opportunities to learn with and from each other

Potentially there can be some significant divisions, particularly between those who continue running training courses and those carrying out consulting. The latter are sometimes seen by the former as staying in expensive hotels, having lots of meetings and not achieving very much. The former are sometimes seen by the latter as working on the margins, also achieving little.

Those internal consultants who are paid by results may well seek to gain and retain a high profile by, for example:

- Supporting a senior manager who is sponsoring a change in IT working processes, by the installation of a major computer system.
- Managing a project that is rolled out company wide and is nominally led by the MD.
- Designing a core set of programmes with external consultants.

These are often the internal consultants that get recognition, gain experience, have credibility and can then secure other high-profile work. They work away from the rest of the team, having or taking little time to share experiences with their colleagues. A two-tier service develops. Team spirit and identity are under severe threat. Here the encouragement of collaboration and shared learning is not just important but vital. Some ways of doing this are:

- Co-training and co-consulting: e.g. training courses can be valuable places for honing skills in managing process; trainers can learn about contracting by working with clients. Having a clear and agreed framework for giving and receiving feedback is vital here.
- Defining opportunities for the movement of staff between training and consulting. There is potentially a lot of rich learning here: e.g. the trainer in joining the consulting team may be able to provide some important first impressions of them and their work.
- Project review meetings where each member of the team brings some of their work for peer supervision; once again the scope for feedback has to be clearly agreed.
- Seminars where team members present on topics of current interest.
- Self-development pairs or groups which are based upon identified strengths, weaknesses and development needs,

e.g. in a pair one person helps the other acquire IT skills in return for learning more about intervention strategies.

- Interteam analysis and feedback. This is based on the assumption that there are some formally agreed subdivisions within the team, e.g. the consulting team responsible for the South-East takes responsibility for helping the North-West team carry out an assessment of their skills. There is then learning not only from the content of the analysis, but the additional, and possibly more important, layer where the South-East team gets feedback on their approach (procedure and process) as consultants and similarly the North-West team can get feedback on their behaviour as clients.
- Risk assessment. Prospective work is assessed by the team before a final decision is made about whether to accept it or not. Various criteria might be used such as:
  - The prospect of the consulting team raising its profile and increasing its influence.
  - The reputation and standing of the client: 'How easy or difficult would they be to deal with?' 'Can they be trusted?'
  - Profitability.
  - Learning, development and excitement within the consulting team.

An interesting variant of this is where one part of the team is briefed to argue *against* taking a piece of work, whilst another argues the case *for*.

- Testing out ideas, interventions and exercises. For example, asking a colleague to role-play a difficult client; using the consulting team for a dummy run in the use of an instrument. Once again there can be learning not only from the content but from many other aspects: the value and appropriateness of instruments; risk levels; validity; timing and briefing.
- Induction of new team members. This can provide excellent opportunities for all concerned:
  - An established member of the team might be asked to

prepare a short presentation (which all can attend) on the organization culture; there is then a chance to compare views.
- The new member might be asked to interview each member of the team and present his/her findings, perhaps under agreed headings, e.g. Relationships (what people see as each other's strengths and weaknesses; what people want and need from each other), Systems (roles and responsibilities, gaps and duplication; the extent to which the technology helps/hinders effective teamwork; rewards and measures of performance), Environment (how the team manages its relationship with customers and other's who have a vested interest in its performance).

Agreeing ways of working
Methods and approaches have to be agreed both *internally* (i.e. within the team) and *externally* (i.e. the team with its clients). There are a number of questions that will need to be considered in each of these areas, e.g.

Internal	*External*
How do we handle conflicts with each other?	How do we clarify and update expectations of each other?
How do we keep each other informed of work and client agreements?	How do we review progress?
How do we support our own learning?	How, if at all, do we disseminate our learning in the rest of the organization?
Where do we direct our efforts?	What specific outcomes does each of us want?
What parts of the business/ clients do we give priority to?	What will be charged for and how?
What form of contracting do	What are the timescales?

we want to adopt with our clients?

How do we handle complaints?

What are the decision points?

What principles, methods and style of working do we want to be known for?

How do we handle differences of view on what needs to be done?

How much freedom does each of us have to contract with clients?

Who does/does not work on this project?

How far can we commit each other's time?

How do we choose a project?

How do we balance revenue generation with personal learning and excitement?

Who are the key players? What is their stance? Do they need to be contracted with?

Who is *our* sponsor? How do we keep her involved and interested? (Or as distant as possible!)

What are the underlying issues we need to consider and how?

What fees do we charge? How far can we vary these, and on what basis?

How far do we want to support/challenge the organization's culture – values, methods and style?

What ethical standards will govern our work, e.g. on issues such as equal opportunities, sexual relationships, supervision, counselling support for self and clients, confidentiality and so on?

Do we arrange to have a friendly critic, not directly involved in the project, who can act as a sounding board?

How far, if at all, do we let the client choose the consultant?

What have we each learnt from the successes and failures we have been involved in both separately and together?

| How do we maintain continuity of service? | What level and type of confidentiality do we maintain and how? |
| How do we arrange handovers? | Who, if anybody, can carry the project forward, if neither of us is available? |

In order for there to be good-quality contracting with clients there, first, has to be good-quality contracting within the team. It is advisable, therefore, that the team answers as many of the internal questions as possible before going to see clients. This is not to say that absolutely everything has to be 'cut and dried' in advance, but that there should be a common understanding in crucial areas. Failure to do so may mean that the consultants are seen as at best, incompetent, and at worst, devious.

Working through such questions may highlight the role and contribution of two parties little mentioned so far: *the consulting team manager* and *the administrative support group*. In the move from training to consulting, the challenges are likely to be as great for the manager as anyone else. Some of these can be:

- *From* scheduler of resources *to* proactive initiator of change.
- *From* detached problem-solver *to* engaged resolver of differences.
- *From* seller of products *to* joint creator.
- *From* expert *to* humble companion in learning.
- *From* naïve realist *to* politician (willing to compromise values, but by how much?).
- *From* backroom academic *to* messy, confident, flawed protagonist.

Such changes of role may have been preceded by a period of uncertainty (falling numbers on training courses, clients questioning the value of training) and some profound self-doubt within the team.

The consulting team manager is likely to be faced with the same personal and business paradoxes as any other worker within the organization. The extra edge is that she may still, rightly or wrongly, be seen as a model for change management. 'If the human resources department cannot get it right who can?' So the manager of the consulting team may be subject to more scrutiny than many others. Inconsistencies between practice and preaching will be quickly noticed. For example, the consultants are less likely to work respectfully through resistance in a client if *their* manager does not do the same for them.

Occasionally in making the transition from training to consulting client work is stopped for several weeks or even months. This does give time for dealing with a lot of the practical and emotional issues described above. However, this is a rarity and most often the planning has to take place in the midst of ongoing work. So the consultants are having to learn how to do their work whilst doing it.

Being an aware learner such as this assumes the capacity and opportunity to step back from a situation. There is less scope for this when working on the absolute edge of and maybe even beyond competence; yet paradoxically this is when it is most needed. The team manager needs an even higher order of skills in both involvement and detachment in order to support learning (e.g. to make sure the double loop learning questions are asked, see Chapter 6). Bearing in mind the 'hall of mirrors' which can be created when two organizational cultures old and new overlay and interact with each other, the manager may well need a high level of honesty with self and others in order to be a source of stability for consultants who after prolonged exposure to the distorting effects of change deep in the organization may become extremely disorientated. The degrees of honesty and openness suggested here may or may not have been part of the tradition of the team.

As mentioned above the other crucial part of the team which I have scarcely mentioned is administrative support. A common definition of an intervention is anything that the consultant does in seeking to influence a part of the system to which he does not belong. I believe therefore that an intervention might not only be, at one extreme, a multi-phased organization development plan but also a phone call answered with anger, excitement, curiosity or indifference. When, therefore, somebody acts on the consultant's behalf (e.g. answering a client query about the current state of a project, training expenses, the quickest route from Bournemouth to Saffron Walden) then those also are interventions. If administrative support answer such questions, they are at that moment acting as the consultant. Their exclusion from team development activities, such as those described above, increase the likelihood of fragmentation developing and becoming apparent to the client. If, as is quite often the case, consultants are brought in to help the client deal with problems of fragmentation then this is not a good advertisement. Setting an example, good or bad, is also an intervention.

Fundamentally, the quality of the consulting team is dependent upon balancing its attention both outwards and inwards. Inwards attention is about relationships, skills and administration systems, but significantly informed by outwards attention:

- What clients are currently saying.
- What is happening in the organization generally.
- What is happening in the market sector.
- Wider global business trends.

It is about nurturing the professional home base, whilst also being very curious about the team's business environment, and not becoming totally preoccupied by either. This is the theme of the case study that follows.

A short illustrative case study

This case study does not seek to describe all aspects of a particular assignment, but simply to identify some crucial features, illustrating earlier points.

An internal Human Resources (HR) group (training, consulting and personnel) was responsible for offering its services on a European-wide basis. The organization as a whole provided financial and linked support services.

A dramatic drop in market share and profitability in the organization meant that the HR group was suddenly faced with many challenges:

- Loss of staff through redundancies.
- Pressure to show they were 'adding value'.
- A sharp dip in course nominations.
- Growing animosity between administrative support, training and personnel.
- Personnel were no longer able to provide services direct (e.g. recruitment) but had to train line managers to fulfil such functions.
- A newly appointed HR director whose remit was to get the HR group performing within six months.

I was asked by the HR director to help.

Phases of the work

1   Interviews with all members of the HR group. This provided confirmation of the anxiety and unsettled atmosphere in the group.
    (*Commentary*. I was particularly keen to establish trust with each member of the group. The time was well spent even though there were no major shocks or significantly new information.)

2   A two-day workshop on consulting skills.
    (*Commentary*. This was an *implicit* intervention in terms of dealing with the animosity and fears. People began to work together in a fairly low-risk way. There was common ground for everybody in the recognized and accepted need to acquire consultancy skills. Development pairs and groups after the workshop helped to maintain momentum. The theoretical content of the workshop was based on content from this book.)

3   A two-day HR strategy workshop. Prior to its taking place, the design was discussed at an open forum. People were invited to volunteer in leading certain sessions. The Managing Director was also invited to attend.

(*Commentary.* The major features in the design which I wanted to achieve were:
- Responsibility being shared around the group.
- Resolving some differences in a relatively safe way – nobody being pushed into confrontation.
- Dealing with external realities, e.g. the MD, business trends.
- Creating an agreed agenda (see Figure 10.3) which could be carried forward.)

Objectives
To contribute to creation of the HR strategy.
To identify ways in which training and personnel might extend areas of collaboration in order to increase the influence of the HR department in the business.

PROGRAMME

8.30	**INTRODUCTION AND SCENE SETTING**
	Overview of the Programme; Objectives; Ground rules (e.g. confidentiality, reasonable openness).
9.30	**TAKING STOCK**
	The World: What do we know/imagine/guess are some of the global influences likely to affect the business over the next 1–5 years?
10.30	**Our Organization:** What do we know/imagine/guess is going on in our organization generally and our stakeholders in particular?
11.30	**HR Group:** What is happening to us?
	a) Personal Styles: Using Belbin to analyse the potential assets and liabilities of particular teams (i.e. training, personnel and administration) and the HR Group as a whole. Each team analyses the other and gives feedback in the full group.
1.00	**Lunch**
2.00–2.30	Using Belbin to analyse the HR Group as a whole.
2.30–4.00	b) Strategic Position: Using analytical and impressionistic exercises to look at the HR Group (see page 134 for illustration).
4.00	**Self:** What does this all mean to me?
	Each participant does an analysis identifying: stakeholders (people who have an investment in their role and performance); their importance (high/medium/low); their

	current satisfaction with the relationship (high/medium/low).
	Pairs/trios discuss points emerging from the exercise and help each other clarify issues and possible action. (NB This is an opportunity for those with stakeholders on the workshop to start problem-solving and resolving differences.)
5.00	**Self-Directed Workshop** (see Appendix II) Participants work on whatever they think would be of benefit to themselves and the group. Some of the many overlapping options:
	– Group Strategy
	– Business Planning
	– Work Organization
	– Product Development
	– Problem-Solving groups/pairs
	– Marketing Training and/or Personnel Services
	– Reflection/Reading/Relaxation
	Participants can add to the list; and might also offer to lead sessions.
6.30	**Workshop Review** Each person reports specifically or generally on what they achieved during the workshop.
7.15	**Identifying Agenda Items for the Following Day** What do we want to achieve tomorrow? (To include planning how to update anyone from the HR Group who is unable to attend.)
8.00	**Dinner**
DAY 2	
8.30–9.30	Managing Director. Presentation of the future of HR in the business.
9.30–10.00	Revisiting and creating the agenda for the day. (This can include any pre-work which has been done regarding individual or team objectives for this off-site meeting.)
10.00–2.30	Implementing the agenda.
2.30–3.00	Updates on progress.
3.00–3.30	Review: outcomes and agreements.

Figure 10.3   Agreed agenda

4   **Postscript.** The second two-day workshop was seen as generally successful:

- Administration and support staff became more assertive:
  - about their own needs, e.g. to be kept informed
  - about their view of the customers' needs (they had excellent networks).
- Recognition by both trainers and consultants that underlying jealousy and rivalry had undermined their joint ability to offer customers a high-quality and consistent service.
- A realization and acceptance of the reality that even with a major marketing campaign there was unlikely to be enough work to sustain the existing members of staff in the HR group. A significant number began planning their departure, strongly believing it made sense to leave at a time of their own choosing.
- The MD had greater respect for the HR group because he saw staff at *all* levels working to understand and capitalize on rapidly changing customer and business requirements.
- A greater willingness of people to accept that they had to be proactive about their development.
- A series of half-day workshops where key customers (identified through stakeholders analysis) were invited to discuss their current perspective on the business and their needs of HR.

However, the continued sharp down trend in business meant that the HR group was always one step behind in restructuring and reinventing itself. The central HR function was largely disbanded and was re-established in a limited way at a local level within the various countries.

Conclusion

Much of what I have described in this chapter is about the management of boundaries: practical and emotional, team and individual, internal and external. As already stated, the work of the team in resolving boundary conflicts and confusions is vital so that they can be effective consultants. However, just like the consultancy cycle, all this is iterative, not linear. It would be naïve for a team to expect to get themselves 'totally sorted out' before undertaking projects. Organizational pressures are not likely to allow it and the nature of the development paths, as described in earlier chapters, means that the move from training to consultancy is sometimes imperceptible. A simple but useful model for aiding the team in stepping back and reviewing its boundaries is based on the work of Stephen Covey.[6] In Figure 10.4 I have slightly modified his model to show three concentric circles.

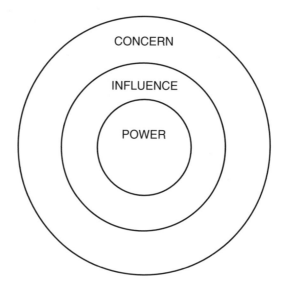

Figure 10.4

The circle of power is where the individual or team can directly make things happen, e.g. reorganize a system, launch a workshop, reallocate roles. The circle of influence is where the individual or team may be able to persuade others to do or agree to something, e.g. extra resources, a completely new focus of work. The circle of concern is where the individual or team need to keep themselves informed, but where they have no direct power or influence, e.g. the composition of the board or market trends. If members of the consulting team have very different views on the nature and sources of their power and influence then they are likely to dissipate their energy, allowing concerns both inside and outside the team to multiply, thus creating a sense of impotence. However, the more a team can reach some collective understanding of where their power and influence lies then this can become a fixed point (albeit temporary) on which to stand and move their world.

Notes

1 Jung, C.G. *Man and his Symbols*, Aldus Books 1964.
2 Egan, G. *Working with the Shadow Side*, Jossey-Bass 1995.
3 Erikson, E. *Identity and the Life Cycle*, W.W. Norton and Co. 1980.
4 Gross, D. *Psychology, the Science of Mind and Behaviour*, Hodder and Stoughton 1992.
5 Dryden, W. *The Handbook of Individual Therapy*, Sage 1996.
6 Covey, S. *The Seven Habits of Highly Effective People*, Simon and Schuster 1992.

11 Consulting from a complexity perspective

Patricia Shaw

Most consultants at some time or another ask themselves the question, what do I really think I'm doing, trying to intervene in the development of something as complex and elusive as an organizational system, with all its myriad and diverse activities. In Chapter 8 we identified some of the models which have helped consultants make sense of their work, many of which come from organization development (OD) and its roots in open systems thinking. More recently thinking about system dynamics has been enriched by the study in a number of different disciplines of the nature of complex networks. This work invites us to probe again some assumptions underlying organization development and the part played by a consultant. In this chapter I will explore some of the implications of these developments.

The OD legacy

Traditionally, the following ideas have informed OD work:

- Organizational systems, be they the whole company or a

department or a team, are open systems seeking a successful 'fit', or dynamic equilibrium, with a changing environment.

- Organizations do this by scanning and analysing the environmental threats and opportunities and simultaneously generating internal aspirations and strategies.
- Senior managers intentionally steer their organizations into a chosen future, through the use of missions, visions and business plans.
- Consultants use a design perspective to help managers develop strategic goals and bring them to fruition.
- Consultants find ways to work with resistance to change, resolving conflicts and developing consensus-based action.

This may seem obvious and uncontroversial. That is the nature of paradigms or widely shared world views. In Chapter 8 we referred to Morgan's seminal work[1] on organizational metaphors. This drew attention to the way our thinking about organizations derives from the natural sciences and the fields of anthropology, sociology and psychology which, whilst being concerned with human systems, have tended to position themselves within the existing scientific paradigm. The ideas of key figures such as Newton, Darwin and Descartes have shaped our thinking so profoundly for three centuries that it is difficult to isolate and question the assumptions underlying the above statements.

Yet, are open systems naturally seeking dynamic equilibrium with their environments? Is it possible to trace cause and effect in complex systems in order to develop strategic direction? How knowable is the future into which senior managers are supposedly steering their organizations? Is it possible to construct ever more accurate representations of an organization and its environment in order to better predict and design the way ahead? It is now becoming clear that a revolution in thinking is shaking the dominant world view that underpins our Western thinking. New discoveries are being made, and previously marginal trains of thought are resurfacing in the mainstream.

The study of complex adaptive systems

One area attracting considerable interest is 'complexity theory' – the study of complex systems in nature, wherever they occur, be it ant colonies, weather patterns, the immune system or the evolution of life. The enormous strides in computer technology of the last 20 years have allowed scientists to simulate the dynamics of network systems comprising very large numbers of intelligent adaptive agents whose interaction is characterized by non-linear feedback processes, that is, when effects are disproportional to the original stimuli.[2] Economists have been using similar ideas to question classical economic theories.[3] Ecologists have been seeking ways to understand the intricate nested networks of the Earth's ecology.[4] At the same time cognitive scientists have been exploring the complex neural networks of the brain,[5] and sociologists and organization theorists are writing about the complex networks of language, knowledge and sense-making that create and sustain all our human institutions.[6]

It is hardly surprising that many consultants working with, for and in organizations are pricking up their ears. Is it possible that describing organizations as highly complex networks could be something more than a lament? As the idea of the web is capturing our collective imagination, so we are beginning to discover much more about the dynamics of adaptive or learning networks.

Some of the principles of relationship, communication and interaction revealed by the study of complex adaptive networks include the following:

1   Such systems are formed by very large numbers of 'agents', each actively making itself by interacting with other agents in its own local context. The agents are interacting with one another according to their own ways of making sense of themselves in their situation. Some of these ways are shared and some are unique to each agent. An agent could be a neuron in the brain or an individual person in a group or a group among other groups or a whole organization

interacting with others in a market economy. This offers a way of understanding the organizational world in terms of intricately nested and overlapping webs of interaction.

2   Agents, each with their own local webs of connection, interact spontaneously giving rise to patterns of activity on larger scales. These patterns emerge from the interaction and also create the conditions in which that interaction takes place. This means that the emerging pattern of activity cannot be predicted from or explained in terms of the behaviour of any single agent.

3   The interaction between agents is non-linear, which means that responses can be multiple and are not proportional to a stimulus so that simple linear cause and effect rapidly disappears. Instead we have loops of amplifying and damping feedback.

4   The specific longer-term development of the network is thus inherently unknowable – it is not a matter of lack of information. No agent or group of agents can be 'in control' of that development.

5   Such networks of agents are creative or, in other words, capable of producing novelty and variety, only when they operate 'at the edge of chaos' or, in other words, at the edge of system disintegration, in paradoxical conditions in which stability and instability coexist. Such system conditions exist *far from equilibrium*, where iterative processes of both amplifying and damping feedback propagate through the system to produce islands of patterned order which arise and dissolve in a sea of disorder.

6   In such conditions, sometimes called bounded instability, novel behaviour, unexpected activities and new patterns of organizing relationships emerge and evolve without any single set of governing rules or blueprints, but through the unfolding logic of self-organizing processes.

The conditions dubbed 'at the edge of chaos' have been a new and interesting discovery – here a complex network is neither falling apart nor ossified. Simulation after simulation reveals some similar characteristics of networks operating in these conditions:

- Agents are richly connected.
- Agents themselves are diverse.
- Information flows rapidly through the network.

Increase these parameters too much, so that there is very little commonality between agents, everyone is connected to everyone else and the network is swamped with information, and the system tips into random behaviour and all order is lost. Reduce these parameters too much so that connections are sparse, the agents are rather similar and information flow is sluggish, and the network becomes 'frozen', capable only of repeating existing patterns. Liveliness and possibly life itself appears to evolve spontaneously to 'edge of chaos' conditions. Santa Fe scientists such as Kauffman speculate that this is the most robust state for a complex dynamical network, where order emerges for free in the midst of disorder.

Human organizations as complex adaptive systems

Stacey argues that social systems can also be thought of as complex adaptive systems, in which agents may be individuals and groups interacting in co-evolving sense-making and action contexts.[7] Peculiarly human characteristics only add to the potential complexity without changing the fundamental dynamics. In particular any organization can be conceptualized in terms of an ordered network of patterned interactions which is intentionally designed – the organization's hierarchical structure of roles and responsibilities, its official policies and processes and its espoused ideology, in the form of explicit missions and culture. As people interact in the designed network, which he calls the legitimate system, they simultaneously and spontaneously spin other networks through entirely self-organizing processes. He calls these the organization's shadow systems and suggests that an organization's evolution can be understood as emerging from all these local network interactions.

What does this mean for the conventional predicting, planning, goal-setting, monitoring and controlling form of management? This becomes relegated to a special and limited case applying to the management of networks operating in stability. Such networks are dominated by damping feedback processes so that repetitive patterns of activity can be reproduced efficiently. The popularity in recent years of the 'softer' forms of control – managing through visions, missions and shared organizational culture – are part of this focus on managing homogeneous and stable systems.

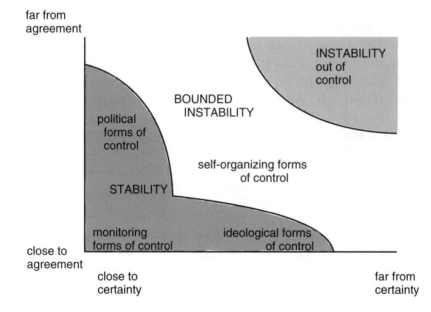

Figure 11.1

Ralph Stacey portrays the situation in Figure 11.1.[8] He argues that much management theory this century has focused on the region of stability when decision-makers are close to certainty about the nature of future developments and are in agreement about what to do about these. In such circumstances it makes sense to gather information, weigh alternatives, set goals and monitor progress against them. He points out that this area of stability can be extended into the region of decreasing agreement by well-known political strategies of negotiation, alliance building and the use of legitimate authority structures. Similarly as the world has seemed ever less predictable the popularity of unifying visions and explicit codes of values intended to 'align' the workforce have gained popularity, keeping agreement in key areas despite increasing uncertainty. Managers have always feared the anarchy of situations where both certainty and agreement collapse into random and disintegrative behaviour. Losing control is many managers' nightmare.

However, what about the border zone that lies between stability and disintegration? The unsettling message from complexity theory is that organizational systems can only produce the creativity, variety and novelty needed to survive in the longer term by operating in this border zone, at the edge of chaos, using a messy process of learning into an unknown and unknowable future. But the messiness need not be the messiness of anarchy that so many managers fear.

It appears that complexity theory is beginning to offer some ways of thinking about the nature of emergence and self-organization and suggesting ways of influencing the conditions that can generate such innovative capability.

The implications for the way development consultants think

Where does all this leave a consultant engaged to help managers with the processes of change and development in organizations? There seem to be two kinds of response. Some consultants (and managers) experience some anger and trepidation believing that the very basis of their work is being undermined. Others notice thoughtfully that this more complex version of organizational life resonates with their experience. They admit to a gap between the official hindsight accounts of most 'change programmes' and the actual messiness and chaos of creative change. Consultants trained in classical organization development who have talked about their work in terms of methodologies for implementing planned change are often all too aware that life never goes according to plan and that some of their best work has been in facilitating the emergence of surprising outcomes, predicted by no one in the unexpected encounters between intention and chance. Being poised ready to work with this is as much a part of their actual practice as the more formal accounts of designed, intentional change programmes.

Could we then begin to articulate some consulting principles that take seriously the description of organizational life that a complexity perspective offers, one that shifts consultants' attention from planned or even plannable change to the messy processes of self-organization and emergent change? There have already been interesting explorations of these ideas by such writers as Nonaka, Pascale, Wheatley, Goldstein and Stacey.[9] My own practice suggests the following principles:

From a traditional perspective, the consultant:	*From a complexity perspective, the consultant:*
Designs and implements an educational strategy to realize planned change intended to improve the organization's position in its environment.	Stimulates conditions of bounded instability in which the organization co-evolves with its environment, through self-organizing processes.
Understands organizational change in terms of transitional instability between *system-wide* stable states.	Understands change dynamics as unfolding in the ongoing tension between coexisting stability and instability, in which islands of order arise and dissolve.
Contracts to deliver a predetermined objective or outcome.	Contracts for an emergent process of complex learning into an evolving and unknowable future.
Sees large-scale project plans and political and ideological control strategies as legitimate	Dissuades managers from using inappropriate forms of control to manage the

ways of realizing prior intention.

anxieties raised when operating far from certainty and agreement.

Chooses an effective marginal or boundary position from which to diagnose the state of the system as a whole and choose interventions.

Becomes an active agent in the life of the organization, by participating in both its shadow and legitimate systems to engage in complex learning processes.

Tries to create an intended change in people's shared beliefs, values and attitudes.

Seeks to stimulate and provoke conditions in which people's co-constructed worlds of meaning are spontaneously revised in interaction.

Focuses on desired global level of system change, and alignment of subsystems – groups, individuals or organizations.

Focuses on feedback loops operating at local level through which activity may be escalated up to unpredictable system-wide outcomes.

Designs and facilitates off-site meetings to build teams and develop strategies and plans.

Intervenes in the ongoing conversational life in organizations in which people continuously create contexts to act into.

Collects data on generic system variables through surveys, interviews and other instruments, to feed back to the system.

Invites an exploration of the relationship between the system's formal agenda (what the legitimate system says it knows) and the multiplicity of informal narratives by which the organization is working (what the shadow system knows). These feedback loops generate their own outcomes.

Emphasizes the need for alignment and consensus around clear direction.

Amplifies existing sources of difference, friction and contention, amidst areas of certainty and agreement.

Implications for the practice of development consultants

The principles outlined above represent a particular stance to organizational consulting work. I will now illustrate how they translate into practice, using an assignment on which I worked with Bill Critchley of Ashridge Consulting Group.

Contracting for unknown outcomes

Previous chapters have emphasized the importance of contracting for clarity around agreed objectives and mutual expectations, but this is not always possible or appropriate when the nature of the assignment is inherently ambiguous. For example, the following are extracts from the tender documentation for a major consulting project in a local authority.

The last few years have been relatively stable. The organisation tends to be bureaucratic, hierarchical, with central controls and is task-oriented. External and internal factors are now driving major changes within the organisation. The recently appointed CEO is a significant influence on the way the organisation responds to change.

Under the chairmanship of the CEO, senior management have been working on a Vision and a corporate management strategy for the many complex issues which the organisation is facing. A copy of the Vision Statement and a copy of a report to the Council entitled 'Facing the Future: Towards a New Approach' are enclosed. One of the many human resource issues they are working on is how to introduce the corporate strategy to the rest of the organisation.

The 'Management of Change' project is concerned with one major element of the corporate strategy, namely to introduce the necessary culture change to ensure that people are working to their potential and feel motivated and empowered to respond to changes . . .

Consultants were asked to submit the following:

- analysis of the organisational needs
- design and development of a culture change programme
- delivery of a culture change programme
- post-evaluation of project and any follow-through work which is necessary

Consultants are required to set out clearly their approaches and methodology under these headings and be able to identify deliverable outputs and timescales for their achievement.

The wording of this document is a good example of the kind of managerial thinking that belongs to the dominant paradigm I referred to above. My colleague and I wrote to explain that we were unable to submit proposals along the lines requested as we thought and worked with a very different perspective in relation to an assignment of this kind, but we would be very happy to discuss this with the tender panel if invited to do so. We enclosed CVs, a relevant article and a few points about the kind of assumptions implicit in the tender material.

During the tender interview we spent a lot of time surfacing the really unanswerable questions that lie behind the conventionally worded rationality of the tender document. As the conversation progressed it became possible to discuss with the panel, which included the Chief Executive Officer (CEO) and several directors, the idea that they did not know what kind of 'organisational culture' they really needed, and that even if they had some vague ideas, culture is impossible to install. Unless, that is, they had in mind nothing more than the promulgation of a set of values, a statement of principles or lists of desirable behaviours. In other words was this a project to inculcate a desired organizational ideology or was it an attempt to enable a creative process of cultural evolution in the organization? If the latter, then participation in the self-organizing processes by which culture is created would be the way we would work, processes in which no one can have overall control.

We purposefully avoided presenting formal proposals that would encourage the idea that there could be many certainties in this kind of project. Instead we introduced a conversational mode in which we kept challenging good-humouredly the conventional management thinking that the panel was espousing, encouraging a frankness about the uncertainty and open-endedness of such an assignment.

We were awarded the contract and it was interesting that the feedback of one of the directors was this: 'Everyone else made presentations based on knowing what to do. You were the only ones that spoke openly about not knowing while still being convincing. It was quite a relief.'

Of course it would be naïve to suppose that the early agreement was a completely blank sheet, but the contract was remarkably open and based on a number of conversations rather than any kind of written document. We undertook initially to:

- Discover and create opportunities to work with the live issues and tasks that were exercising people formally and informally in the organization.
- Use these opportunities to 'catch' critical incidents revealing of the organizational culture as they happened and to invite reflection on these.
- Let these activities develop their own consequences and implications for further work.
- Meet with the CEO, and whoever else he or the consultants wished to invite or who invited themselves, to make emergent sense out of the work.

A daily rate was agreed, but the overall budget for the project remained unknown to us. We decided not to enquire, but to allow the ongoing question about how value-for-money could be assessed to be repeatedly explored as the project developed.

In order to produce some sort of picture of how the assignment might unfold we produced the diagram in Figure 11.2

which helped to soothe everyone's nervousness, even though on close inspection it is not very specific. The challenge of the early contracting phase was to deal creatively with the tensions between clarity and ambiguity, intentionality and uncertainty, purposefulness and open-endedness.

Phase 1:   **Engaging with the organization**
Raising awareness of the culture –
how is it sustained in day-to-day interaction?

 Individuals

Special forums

Teams and working groups

Phase 2:   **Working with and creating more purposeful groups**
and forums as issues and themes become clearer –
seeing opportunities for change

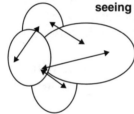

Seeding into many levels of the organization

Connecting people and groups

Mobilizing energy, interest, participation, motivation, responsibility

Phase 3:   **Harnessing the momentum for change**

Facilitating steering/coordinating groups

Helping particular groups to take forward learning and action in specific areas

NB Although this may look linear, it is not. The work phases overlap and do not have sharp starting and ending points.

Figure 11.2   Culture change assignment

Taking up a role in both the legitimate and shadow networks

As consultants we believed we needed two things:

- A clear role in the formal organization.
- Freedom to interact spontaneously in the informal or shadow organization.

This was achieved by the CEO writing a letter to all staff which was enclosed with their pay statements, introducing us to the organization and explaining our role and accountabilities. The letter published our telephone numbers and invited any member of staff to contact us to suggest areas of work or people we should meet. We also asked for copies of the internal telephone directory and said we would start two kinds of work simultaneously. We would arrange to talk with directors and others that the CEO wanted us to meet. We would also take our own initiative in wandering around the organization, making our own connections and following up on contacts as we saw fit.

We were given passes to facilitate our free movement around the organization and were thus in an ambiguous category that was helpful to our work – we were and were not members of the organization. We had a legitimate role with contractual responsibilities and accountabilities, albeit temporary, like any member of staff and we rapidly acted so as to become members of the many informal networks of contacts and relationships operating in the organization.

It was made explicit with the client that he would be paying for the time needed for us to become active participants in the life of the organization. We had the freedom to begin work without a prior plan of action or his prior approval. The issue of control was explored in the following ways:

- We could be asked to discuss our work at any time.
- No work would be possible without the parties concerned being interested in involving us as they would not be under any obligation to do so.

- The grapevine would carry diverse information about our activities that would both enable and constrain the work in a dynamic and evolving way.
- The CEO would use both informal and formal channels of communication to track opinion on what was happening.

We were letting go of the consulting model explained in Chapter 4, in order to experiment collaboratively with our clients to evolve other ways of working. It was clear that there would be no data collection, diagnosis or feedback in the usual sense of these terms. There would be no attempt to define either an existing or a new culture to be implemented in some way, but to facilitate the spontaneous emergence of novel patterns of activity.

Intervening in a complex adaptive network

Where does one start intervening in a large and complex organization with an enormous range of activities? Rather than agonize over this question, we decided to ask the organization itself. We seized the opportunity when meeting one of the sub-editors of a recently inaugurated employee newsletter, to ask him to insert a last-minute item just before the next edition went to press. This was headed 'Can we talk?' and explained the dilemma facing us. We said that we would be sitting in a certain room at certain times and invited anyone who saw themselves as involved or interested in shaping or changing the way the organization worked, in however small or large a way, to simply turn up.

On the first occasion we waited for ten minutes in an empty room with a trolley full of coffee wondering whether anyone would come. Six people did. Next time there were only 2, then 18, 14, 12 and 22. Each time people were encouraged to tell the story of how they came to be at this meeting and the groups were invited to discuss the cultural patterns they perceived.

By the last occasion, some 75 people had come to the meetings and someone said, 'Wouldn't it be good if there were 100 of us'. Thus the seeds of what became the 100 Forum were sown, the nature of the 'us' remaining usefully ambiguous. A note to those who had responded to the 'Can we talk?' invitation, and to the few who had called or had met us on our wanderings, announced the creation of a forum for communication and participation about the way the organization was and was not changing. It was open to anyone to come if they wanted and to bring or influence others to come. Again we waited with more coffee in a large hall we had located. Some 60 people drifted in over the first 20 minutes and milled around talking and drinking coffee. Circles of chairs had been arranged in small groups and people sat down to discuss with each other what they thought the Forum was for. After 30 minutes half the members of each group left and joined other groups and continued the conversation. This was repeated twice more and then we asked people to say what was emerging. We logged up the range of aspirations, frustrations, questions, demands and suggestions that arose in the larger group conversation. We left the inevitable 'what happens now?' question to be answered by the group. People wanted to publish the material, as it was, in the newsletter. Others wanted to set up informal groups to explore various things. Others wanted another Forum meeting. Others wanted to invite certain people to the next Forum.

Over the following year the Forum met eight times, with an ever-shifting population of people involved, including street cleaners, councillors, managers, teachers, secretaries, the mayor, architects, librarians, the CEO and many others. It slowly evolved a variety of structures and purposes.

Facilitating self-organizing processes

When we first became involved with the organization a number of task forces and working parties had been established to explore and report on change initiatives in employee communication, the introduction of a new performance management system, compulsory competitive tendering, customer service, employee safety, devolution of authority, and so on. These groups were a mini-organizational hierarchy in themselves, with different levels of power and priority revealed by the position of the chair in each case. They were all beavering away producing reports and proposals for consideration by the senior management team. We became involved with a number of these groups, by joining some of their meetings and by holding some meetings open to members of any and all the various groups. We kept asking those involved what they thought they were doing, what assumptions they might be making about their work and what joint meaning they were creating together.

Over a period of some months interesting developments took place. Members of the formal task forces and working parties who were briefed to design and recommend the 'what' and 'how' of change interacted much more with each other and other individuals and interest groups. As a result some of the original groups 'died', others split into subgroups, people co-opted themselves on to groups, membership of some groups reached further into the organizational hierarchy, leadership changed, other interest groups came into being. At the fifth meeting of the Forum a map of all the groups at work on various issues was created. People discussed the links they saw with other groups, the difficulties they were experiencing, and the progress they were making. The sense of a very active network of activity became evident. The CEO who was at this Forum was surprised and delighted. Talking with us afterwards it was clear that he found it hard to understand how the switch from the original formalized structure of groups producing reports to a network of activity had happened – it was unplanned. 'We must capitalize on this,' he enthused. 'I shall appoint someone to co-ordinate and capture the work of these groups.' Then he paused and said 'OK. I think I've got it. This is what you have meant by self-organization – I don't need to appoint a co-ordinator because these groups are co-ordinating themselves.'

Over the next few months the 'structure' of groups that had emerged became firmer and the change network acquired a quasi-official status with a core group and a broader periphery. After the sixth meeting of the Forum members of the change network said that they would take over its organization and facilitation. They started taking the Forum out to other venues and changed its name to the Exchange.

Throughout this time the focus of the consultants was to help create conditions that might stimulate the self-organizing potential of the organization by 'tuning up' the key parameters of connectivity, diversity and the flow of information and sense-making in the organizational networks. In human systems issues of power and anxiety in the face of uncertainty are also key and we tried to sustain the Forum in the tension between exciting/disturbing ambiguity and supporting/containing structures. It was a place where paradoxically, although people held different amounts of power, no one person was in control over who came or over what happened there. It was only possible to influence the process by participating in it.

It is also important to note that although the Forum was a visible manifestation of our activities, we were working all the time with the feedback loops generated by the existence of the Forum. Incidents that arose there sometimes spawned ripples of concern that spread like wildfire to kick in strong damping responses that reined in the possibility of change. In these cases we invited reflection on the repetitive patterns that people could recognize occurring and how everyone was playing a part in sustaining these. At other times, a small encounter or seed of an idea grew through unexpected amplifying feedback processes into major outcomes no one had foreseen.

An example of this was the production of an in-house play on communication in the organization which began as an idea within the employee communications team to illustrate a report to the management team using a few vignettes of organizational life. With encouragement this idea grew to involve a scriptwriter and several actors who worked with a number of groups in the organization, including one of the Forum sessions, to create material from peoples' stories of their working experience. This became a very provocative and well-staged piece of theatre that was given 20 performances for staff from all over the organization. It was followed, both after the performance and in working groups and teams during the ensuing weeks, by discussions and workshops that explored the issues raised. Thus a small beginning escalated to produce a rather unusual form of development activity in a matter of months, while a more formal and traditional approach to organizing training and development was still working its way through various design and planning stages.

Since the links between cause and effect are rapidly lost in a non-linear feedback system operating far from equilibrium, it is impossible to predict how small incidents may be escalated up to major consequences or damped down to create negligible effect. I would argue that it is impossible to know in advance what will turn out to be significant in the longer term or what kind of significance that will be. It therefore makes little sense to look for levers of change – a profoundly Newtonian idea. Instead, I suggest, consultants must risk fanning, rather than controlling or steering, what is happening, to keep a system moving away from equilibrium where the presence of amplifying and damping feedback loops can do their own creative work.

Some final reflections

I have briefly illustrated here, with reference to a culture change project, what can happen when consultants dissatisfied with traditional forms of planned change start operating from a complexity perspective. I believe that this provides a further development path when the distinctions so important in creating the structure of the earlier parts of the book start to dissolve as consultants gain experience and face the irreducible complexities of organizational change and development. The complexity perspective brings a fresh impetus, rigour and coherence to the thinking and skills of consultants with a systems orientation who have been using the following ideas for years:

- Self-similar patterns exist at different scales of any complex dynamical system.
- Paradox and contradiction are essential stimuli for creativity.
- Networks of relationship are the crucibles of change.
- Small interventions can have very large consequences and vice versa.

The perspective I am introducing here suggests how consultants can find ways to think about their active participation in the endlessly unfolding narratives of complex change. This book has carefully constructed distinctions and also questioned these, letting some of them dissolve. This mirrors something of the nature of any development path. For many it is experienced as a cyclical journey in which frameworks and skills which initially helped start to hinder and have to collapse to enable fresh integrations to be made, while ideas abandoned along the way return in a new guise. Order and chaos, stability and instability have to keep interacting for learning and creativity to occur.

Notes

1   Morgan, G. *Images of Organization*, Sage 1997.
2   Goodwin, B. *How the Leopard Changed its Spots*, Weidenfield and Nicholson 1994; Holland, J. *Adaptation in Natural and Artificial Systems*, University of Michigan Press 1975; Kauffman, S.A. *At Home in the Universe*, Oxford University Press 1995; Waldrop, M.M. *Complexity: the Emerging Science at the Edge of Chaos*, Simon and Schuster 1992.
3   Arthur, B. 'Increasing Returns and the Two Worlds of Business', *Harvard Business Review*, 1995.
4   Lovelock, J. *Gaia: the Practical Science of Planetary Medicine*, Gaia Books 1991.
5   Varela, J., Thompson, E. and Rosch, E. *The Embodied Mind: Cognitive Science and Human Experience*, MIT Press 1991.
6   Minges, J. *Self-Producing Systems: Implications and Applications of Autopoiesis*, Plenum Press 1995; Tsoukas, H. 'Forms of Knowledge and Forms of Life in Organised Contexts', in R. Chia (ed.) *In the Realm of Organization: Essays for Robert Cooper*, Routledge 1996; Weick, K.E. *Sensemaking in Organisations*, Sage 1995.
7   Stacey, R. *Complexity and Creativity in Organisations*, Berrett-Koheler 1996.
8   Stacey, ibid.
9   Goldstein, J. *The Unshackled Organisation: Facing the Challenge of Unpredictability through Spontaneous Reorganisation*, Productivity Press 1994; Nonaka, I. 'Creating Order Out of Chaos: Self-Renewal in Japanese Firms', *California Management Review*, Spring 1988, pp. 57–73; Pascale, R. *Managing on the Edge: How Successful Companies Use Conflict to Stay Ahead*, Viking 1990; Stacey, R. *Complexity and Creativity in Organisations*, Berrett-Koehler 1996; Wheatley, M.J. *Leadership and the New Science: Learning about Organisation from an Orderly Universe*, Berrett-Koehler 1992.

Appendix I Getting started: a self-development plan for trainers

The model in Figure A.1 indicates four interlinked areas for learning. They are not mutually exclusive; development in one will inevitably affect the other three.

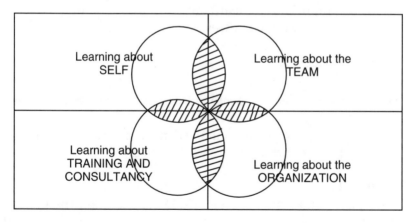

Figure A.1

Self

- The capacity to handle uncertainty and ambiguity with confidence and competence requires a willingness to learn about self, i.e. personal style, values, beliefs and preferences.

Training and consultancy

- A need to learn about, design and run more flexible and experientially based events/sessions/workshops.
- The ability to move out of the training room.
- Learning how to encourage self-development.
- Learning how to manage relationships with a client.

Team

- The team is an important source of stability, support and strategy.
- It can provide a living model of how to work in a collaborative way.
- It is important to learn about individual and collective strengths and weaknesses.

Organization

- Taking a wider perspective; learning to see the organization as an entity.
- Seeing the organization in the context of a changing environment; discovering the trends which affect it.

Methods

The plan contains a variety of different learning methods. In this way you can familiarize yourself with your own preferred way of learning and its assets and liabilities. Some examples of the methods are: guided reading, projects, direct feedback from colleagues, short self-study programmes, course attendance, mentoring, coaching, conducting interviews/surveys; indeed any everyday occurrence can be seen as an opportunity for learning.

Detailed outline

Under each of the four areas there are suggested activities. The first step in developing an individual plan may be the generation of ideas in each of the areas.

Self

Planning time for self-development

- Keep a time log. Decide how much time you will allocate for your own development; begin to set some priorities.
- Complete a computer-based package on time management.
- Read some books on time management.[1]

Gaining greater self-awareness

- Tape a training session; use it to carry out a self-assessment which you can then discuss with a colleague.
- Complete a self-awareness questionnaire, e.g. transactional analysis,[2] Myers-Briggs.[3]
- Complete a learning styles inventory.[4]
- Stretch yourself by taking risks during training sessions, e.g. being more confronting or supportive; less directive.
- Attend some personal development programmes.
- Keep a journal of your thoughts and feelings; review it over time and identify any themes.
- Find a co-counselling[5] partner and arrange regular sessions. Use this as an opportunity to explore your feelings and to identify common themes in your work and life.
- Consider engaging in some professional counselling or therapy in order to increase your understanding of yourself.

Assessing your support networks

- Consider the type of support you currently get and from whom – emotional closeness, intellectual stimulation, professional challenge, fun. Assess whether it is adequate for your current needs; where and how you might change and extend it.

Training and consultancy

Knowledge of the variety of self-development techniques

- Get together with some colleagues to brainstorm some ideas.
- Do some reading on self-development[6] and action learning.[7]
- Join or form a self-development group or action learning set.

Knowledge of consultancy

- Assess yourself against a consulting skills checklist (see Appendix III).
- Read some books on consultancy.[8]
- Find out who does consultancy in your section/organization; go and interview them to find out what they do and the skills they use.
- Arrange to go out with a consultant as an observer on a client visit.
- Conduct some interviews to practise your data collection skills.

Development of design to incorporate self-development techniques

- Take a session on an existing course and redesign it so that the participants are more responsible for deciding the learning content, while the trainer managers the overall structure.

- Practise having a day of self-directed workshops on standard courses.
- Design pre- and post-course briefing materials.
- Help a colleague formulate a self-development plan.
- Carry out a post-course counselling session with a manager; follow it with some self-supervision.

Discovering how training and consultancy are carried out in other organizations

- Think of some organizations which are similar to yours and others which are very different; arrange to visit some of them.
- Arrange a short period of secondment or an exchange.
- Co-train or co-consult with people from other organizations.
- Network; join your local branches of associations and professional bodies, e.g. AMED,[9] IPD,[10] attend conferences.

Team

Knowledge of your team role

- Complete an inventory on team roles;[11] discuss with your team how your roles relate to each other and the implications for team effectiveness.
- Undertake an assignment which requires your team to work together; use the model of task, procedure and process to review your effectiveness.
- Videotape some of your meetings.
- Invite a consultant to help you review the way you work.

Working with other members of the team

- Create opportunities to work on each other's courses; run some sessions jointly.

- Take time to get to know each other's differences and similarities; arrange a half-day where each member of the team writes down on flipchart their skills and experience, what they can offer and what they want from their colleagues. Post these round the room and negotiate wants and offers.

Using the team as a resource base

- Draw up a chart of the organizational networks, both formal and informal, with which each member of the team is in touch.
- Develop a system whereby members of the team can gather and share information about the organizational changes which are taking place.

Organization

Knowledge of organizational models

- Reading.[12]
- Carry out an organizational diagnosis (see Chapter 8).

Learning about the organization's environment

- Interview some senior managers.
- Read the newspapers over a fortnight and draw up a mind map which incorporates the main news items which affect your organization.
- Read in-house journals, abstracts and annual reports.
- Interview members of the public for their views on your organization or the business sector it represents.
- Arrange a visit to one of the client companies of your organization.
- Find out if anybody in your organization is carrying out an organization culture survey.

Being a resource link to the organization

- Review the information which your department receives regularly.
- Discuss with your colleagues ways in which the dissemination of the information could be used to promote training and consultancy.
- Visit other departments and sites within the organization; become 'visible'.
- Explore the possibilities of collaboration with other training and consultancy establishments.
- Identify and build informal influential contacts; discover from them how training and consultancy might be of added value to the organization.

Notes

1 Garratt, S. *Managing Your Time*, Fontana 1984.
2 Available from Mike Reddy, 90 Church Rd, Woburn Sands, Bucks MK17 8TR.
3 Keirsey, D. and Bates, M. *Please Understand Me – Character and Temperament Types*, Prometheus Nemesis Book Co. 1984.
4 Available from Peter Honey and Alan Mumford, MCB University Press Ltd, Human Resource Studies, 62 Toller Lane, Bradford BD8 9BY.
5 Heron, J. *Co-counselling Teachers Manual*, Human Potential Research Project, University of Surrey 1978.
6 Pedler, M., Burgoyne, J. and Boydell, T. *A Manager's Guide to Self Development*, McGraw-Hill 1978.
7 Pedler, M. (ed.) *Action Learning in Practice*, Gower 1983.
8 Lippitt, G. and Lippitt, R. *The Consulting Process in Action*, University Associates.
9 Association for Management Education and Development, 14–15 Belgrave Square, London SW1X 8PS. Tel. 0171 235 3505. Fax. 0171 235 3565.
10 Institute of Personnel and Development, IPD House, Camp Rd, Wimbledon SW19 4UW.
11 Belbin, R.M. *Management Teams: Why They Succeed or Fail*, Heinemann 1981.
12 Handy, C. *Understanding Organizations*, Penguin 1976.

Appendix II Setting up and running self-directed workshops*

As training and development (T and D) departments seek to be more responsive to their customers' needs, there is a growing recognition of the need for flexibility in learning methods. In our experience there are many within T and D who want to stop running training courses altogether and concentrate more on tailor-made activities such as counselling, coaching, team-building, facilitating staff meetings, setting up mentoring contracts and organizing distance learning resources.

However, managers are quite often reluctant to see the total disappearance of training courses and one response by T and D has been the use of self-directed workshops. These can be defined as specific periods of time (lasting hours or even days) within a training course when participants are given responsibility for organizing and using the resources necessary to meet their chosen learning goals. The subject matter could be technical, such as learning how to use some new computer software,

---

* This is an expanded extract from 'A Practical Guide to Self Development' by Keri Phillips and Annette Bradley. Previously published in *The Training Officer*, Vol 29, No 4, 1993.

but we have found there is usually a greater emphasis on people skills, with opportunities to learn about, for example, teamwork, motivation, leadership, appraisal. The reason for this seems to be that self-directed workshops provide a laboratory where participants can experience and analyse a whole range of behaviours and feelings closely associated with people development. During the workshop they may well feel highly motivated, irritated, be hungry for leadership, enjoy working in a team, and so on.

Whilst self-directed workshops can be rewarding and exciting, they require some managing by the trainers. It can be easy to go either to the extreme of abdication, or of manipulative control as in, 'Are you really sure you don't want to do something on motivation?' (The trainer has her favourite motivation exercise which she is keen to use.) In broad terms it means balancing permission and protection.[1] Freedom for people to make their own decisions about what and how they want to learn, whilst also setting limits. This is reflected in the specific suggestions below.

Suggested ground rules for participants
Participants should:

- Concentrate on what they want to do.
- Take the initiative for getting what they want.
- Say if something is not working for them. They may then seek to influence their colleagues to change. Alternatively they might choose to move on elsewhere, setting up or joining a new activity.
- Manage their time well and keep to time commitments.
- Ask for help if they need it.
- Log on a displayed timetable what they are doing and when; this timetable should be updated when necessary.

Suggested procedure

1   The trainer sets the scene, that is, gives a rationale for self-directed learning (an opportunity to experience working in

a flatter structure and focusing on specific individual needs); mentions the ground rules and outlines the procedure; the trainer may also mention the areas which might be worked on and the resources available. Whilst respecting confidentiality, reference to specific individuals and issues which have already arisen is usually more effective than referring to a topic (Contrast 'You Sandra said yesterday you had problems managing your boss so you might want to look at that' with 'Some of you might be interested in assertiveness. There is a package at the back of the room'). It is also valuable if the trainer mentions some of the methods which could be used, for example counselling, brainstorming groups, guided reading, role-plays, and so on. It is vital for the trainer to be very clear about her role; what help she is willing to give, and when.

2   Individuals spend perhaps 20 minutes reflecting on what they want to do, for example, 'Consider how to make my team more effective', 'Learn about counselling', 'Prepare for a presentation to my boss'. It is better if the trainer discourages discussion at this stage, otherwise people may tend to follow rather than assert their own needs.

3   Each person declares what they want to do. The trainer and others may do some probing in order to help clarify the need, but it is important not to go into too much detail otherwise the planning pre-empts the workshop itself. The trainer is advised to encourage others to make offers, for example, 'Is anybody willing to role-play Sandra's boss?', and declare shared interests, for example 'Is there anybody else who wants to join Bill in learning about appraisal?' However, the trainer should not try to organize everybody. This is, firstly, because the logistics are probably too complex for one person to manage, and, secondly, the participants are there to share responsibility.

4   After the declarations people finalize their agreements through informal discussions, and begin filling in the timetable. This is preferably drawn up on a whiteboard and consists of names, including the trainer's, and time slots. Using a whiteboard means that the initial chaos can be easily

accommodated as people begin logging and then amending their sessions as they discover that, for example, Jean cannot do the role-play because she is already booked to work with John. The trainer must stand back from all this and allow the participants to make their own arrangements. The trainer is not responsible for making sure that everybody gets all their needs met. Participants may have to make some difficult decisions about priorities and whose needs are more important. The trainer should, however, keep an eye open for anybody who seems to be uninvolved – this will be evident by the blank spaces against their name on the time-table – and find out what the problem is. The trainer may agree to take part in certain activities or offer to run some sessions, but she will find it useful to keep some time free to monitor the total event. If there is more than one trainer, then this responsibility can be shared.

5   Sometimes, particularly if a long time (more than four hours) has been allocated for the workshop, or the trainer has some doubts about the willingness or ability of the participants, then it can be helpful to have regular reviews. Here the total group comes together to discuss whether the workshop is being successful and what actions may need to be taken. A statement of the obvious, but there is usually a lot of learning when things apparently go wrong. With self-directed work-shops it is often because participants are not really taking responsibility. This is a useful lesson for those needing to be more effective in flatter structures.

6   After the workshop the trainer has an opportunity to run a very rich session where participants discuss the content of what they learned, for example, Sandra describes her plan for managing her boss more effectively, and the process of self-directed learning, for instance, 'How easy did people find it to take responsibility and what are the implications for back at work?' Sometimes people will have got very deeply involved in the workshop and they can be helped to wind out of it and prepare for the review simply by being given a few minutes each to describe some of the feelings they have experienced.

Self-directed workshops are not a soft option for the trainer but require careful preparation and management. In this, the issues which arise may be a microcosm of dilemmas facing the company as a whole: how to generate initiative and creativity whilst focusing on and achieving organizational objectives.

Note

1 Crossman, P. 'Permission and Protection', *Transactional Analysis Bulletin*, Vol. 5, No. 19, 1966.

Appendix III A checklist of consultant competences

Below we list some key areas of effectiveness for a consultant, divided under three main headings:

- Personal and interpersonal effectiveness.
- Working as an agent of change.
- Consulting skills.

The checklist is intended to guide personal reflection in identifying development needs. It can also be used for self- and peer-assessment.

Personal and interpersonal effectiveness

1   *Self-knowledge:* awareness of the values and beliefs that influence the way I work. Awareness of my own motivations and the personal rewards I derive from consulting. Awareness of the ethical choices I do, and would, make when faced with difficult, conflicting options.
2   *Self-awareness:* awareness of my own emotional response to

215

situations and people, particularly awareness of patterns which may lead to inflexible behaviour.

3   *Active listening:* attending to the content and process level in communication. Being attuned to non-verbal signals and their possible meaning. Ability to draw others out. Diagnosing possible underlying feelings, concerns and motivations.

4   *Self-expression:* ability to express my own thoughts, ideas and feelings clearly. Awareness of incongruities in my verbal and non-verbal expression.

5   *Relationship-building:* building open, collaborative relationships. Exchanging feedback in a timely and constructive way. Being assertive, when appropriate, particularly with authority figures. Balancing support and challenge in relationships. Ability to influence others and gain commitment. Being open to influence from others.

6   *Conflict-handling:* valuing and exploring differences. Ability to challenge without alienating. Maintaining flexibility, choice and self-esteem when faced with conflict and hostility. Having the personal courage to open up potentially difficult areas.

7   *Personal and professional limits:* awareness of the limits of my own competence. Willingness to ask for help. Willingness to admit my own mistakes without loss of self-confidence. Commitment to my ongoing development.

Working as an agent of change

8   *Tolerance of ambiguity:* ability to live with uncertainty and complexity without undue stress. Searching for meaning without grasping at over-simplistic interpretations or rushing into premature action. Tolerating incompleteness.

9   *Maintaining a long-term perspective:* helping clients identify and articulate desired futures. Setting short- and medium-term goals in the light of a longer-term sense of purpose.

10   *Maintaining a wide perspective:* attending to the wider context of my work. Not drawing boundaries too tightly.

Dealing with each subsystem's interaction with its supra-system. Keeping abreast of trends and developments in organizational, business and world affairs.

11 *Understanding the nature of change:* developing an intellectual and experiential understanding of change processes – how and why people change, how and why they avoid change, how larger systems change or avoid changing.

12 *Facilitating change:* encouraging widespread participation in the design and implementation of change. Supporting others through the stress of transition. Being aware of myself as a catalyst and seeing the possibilities of intervention in all aspects of my work and interaction with clients.

Consulting skills

13 *Agreeing working contracts:* clarifying mutual expectations and responsibilities. Renegotiating the terms of my work when necessary.

14 *Data collection:* choosing appropriate methods of data collection. Asking pertinent questions. Formulating useful questions. Encouraging client ownership of data.

15 *Diagnosis:* having a range of frameworks and models for understanding individuals, groups and organizations. Maintaining a critical approach to models. Ability to construct my own models. Encouraging joint diagnosis with my clients.

16 *Design:* being creative and purposeful in designing interventions. Not relying on packaged, favourite interventions. Being willing to redesign on the spot. Designing at the level of content and process simultaneously.

17 *Closure:* disengaging well from assignments. Avoiding mutual dependency with my clients. Reviewing learning from each project.

Suggested reading

The following list of books and articles is divided into four sections corresponding to the main themes of this book. These are:

- The trends of change.
- From training to consulting.
- From training to learning.
- From individual to organizational change.

We have already referred to some of the titles; others provide additional ideas in each area.

The trends of change

The Age of Unreason, C. Handy (Hutchinson 1989). Argues for new concepts of work, organizations, society and education.
The Empty Raincoat, C. Handy (Hutchinson 1994). Identifies the paradoxes of our times and explores their implications for corporations and society.

Our World in Transition, D. O'Murchu (Temple House Books 1992). Attempts to make sense of a changing world. Includes many useful tables identifying the direction of changes.

Rethinking the Future, R. Gibson (ed.) (Nicholas Brealey 1997). Leading organizational theorists and practitioners rethink business, competition, control and complexity leadership, markets and the world.

When Corporations Rule the World, D.C. Korten (Earthscan 1996). An acclaimed account of the challenges facing the ever more powerful corporate entities in a global economy.

The Revolution in Managerial Careers, P. Herriot and C. Pemberton (John Wiley 1996). A consideration of the fundamental changes affecting aspirations and opportunities in organizations.

Managing on the Edge, R.T. Pascale (Penguin 1991). Pascale argues that conflict within organizations is not only unavoidable but highly desirable and capable of generating creative tension. Supported by case studies of several corporations, the author shows how this creative tension can be maintained to help organizations transform themselves.

Talking from 9 to 5, D. Tannen (Virago 1995). Tannen outlines how our gender affects our expectation of, and our behaviour in, communicating with each other within organizations. The persistence of the 'glass ceiling' is scrutinized, as are the ways in which our conversational style can limit or enhance our promotion prospects.

The Adaptive Corporation, A. Toffler (Pan/Gower 1985). Uses a major study of AT&T (the American Telephone and Telegraph Company) to describe and comment on organizational response to changes in the environment.

Reinventing the Corporation, J. Naisbitt and P. Aburdene (Macdonald 1985). Describes some of the major social trends and their implications for managing organizations.

The Change Masters, R.M. Kanter (Counterpoint 1985). The result of research carried out in 'successful' and 'unsuccessful' organizations. A blend of theory and case study material.

In Search of Excellence, T.J. Peters and R.H. Waterman (Harper and Row 1982). The bestseller which spawned a number of 'excellence' books and which describes key factors for organizational success such as being close to the customer and entrepreneurship.

Information and Organizations, Max Boisot (Fontana 1987). Looks at the structure of information and information sharing and implications for communication strategies.

From training to consulting

Flawless Consulting: A Guide to Getting Your Expertise Used, P. Block (Learning Concepts 1981). An excellent, practical, well-written book with useful guidelines and checklists.

High Income Consulting, T. Lambert (Nicholas Brealey 1995). A simple guide to running a consultancy.

Helping the Client, J. Heron (Sage 1990). Challenging and interesting models on consultancy style and their implications.

Client-centred Consulting, P. Cockman, B. Evans and P. Reynolds (McGraw-Hill 1992). A practical guide for internal advisers and trainers.

Improving Trainer Effectiveness, R. Bennett (ed.) (Gower 1988). A collection of papers reviewing the changing role of trainers.

'Tomorrow's Industrial Training Officer: the Challenge of Change', E. Donnelly, *Journal of European Industrial Training*, Vol. 9, No. 5, 1985. Traces the historical development of the training role and suggested trends for the future.

'Patterns and Paradoxes of Trainers' Careers: the Implications for the Influence of Training', J. Davies, *Journal of European Industrial Training*, Vol. 9, No. 2, 1985. Research which identifies different trainer roles and self-concepts and their consequences for trainers and organizations.

'Training for Change: A Case-study of the Trainer's Role', M. Walton, *Journal of European Industrial Training*, Vol. 10, No. 4, 1986. Uses a case study to illustrate the difference between trainer/consultant roles.

From training to learning

The Fifth Discipline, P. Senge (Century Books 1990). A seminal book on learning in organizations.

The Learning Company, M. Pedler, J. Burgoyne and T. Boydell (McGraw-Hill 1991). Includes many ideas and exercises for approaching organizational learning.

Business as a Learning Community, R. Lessem (McGraw-Hill 1993). Integrates seminal learning concepts from key writers of recent years.

Mentoring in Action, D. Clutterbuck and D. Megginson (Kogan Page 1995). A comprehensive overview of theory and practice.

Transformational Mentoring, J. Hay (McGraw-Hill 1995). A detailed look at the interpersonal aspects of mentoring and the developmental relationship.

Resource Based Learning, J. Dorrell (McGraw-Hill 1993). A review of the methods and approaches available for establishing flexible learning in organizations.

Total Quality Learning, R. Lessem (Blackwell 1991). The theory and practice of creating a learning organization. It also includes a less well known learning styles inventory.

Self-Development – A Facilitator's Guide, D. Megginson and M. Pedler (McGraw-Hill 1992). An examination of roles and specific interventions for developers within organizations.

'Developing within the Organization: Experiences of Management Self Development Groups', M. Pedler, *MEAD*, Vol. 17, Part 1, Spring 1986. Describes an MSC-funded project to research the outcomes and benefits of membership of self-development groups in a number of organizations.

'Promoting Natural Learning Activities within the Organization', T.N. Garavan, *Journal of European Industrial Training*, Vol. 11, No. 7, 1987. Describes development as the joint responsibility of managers and T & D specialists.

'Using Reality in Management Development', A. Mumford, *MEAD*, Vol. 18, Part 3, Autumn 1987. A call to use managers' everyday reality for 'live' management development.

'Management Learning Contracts: From Theory to Practice', G.

Boak and M. Stephenson, *Journal of European Industrial Training*, Vol. 11, No. 4, 1987 and Vol. 11, No. 6, 1987. Describes the ingredients of a learning contract.

'How "Self" Directed is Self Directed Learning?', G. Robertson, *MEAD*, Vol. 18, Part 2, Summer 1987. A challenging review of the values and assumptions behind self-development.

The Learning Organization, B. Garratt (Fontana/Gower 1987). A guide to the development of directors to promote their own learning and that of the companies they lead.

From individual to organizational change

A Strategy of Change, D.C. Wilson (Routledge 1992). Concepts and controversies in the management of change.

Managing Change in Organizations, C. Carnall (Prentice Hall 1995). An up-to-date review of theory and practice.

What Makes Consultancy Work, R. Casemore, G. Dyos, A. Eden, K. Kellner, J. McAuley and S. Moss (eds) (South Bank University Press 1994). A collection of papers from practising consultants on the dynamics of organizational change.

New Thinking in Organizational Behaviour, H. Tsoukas (ed.) (Butterworth-Heinemann 1994). An excellent collection of papers on recent thinking.

Metaphor and Organizations, D. Grant and L. Oswick (eds) (Sage 1996). A wide-ranging review of the metaphors of organization and organizing.

Strategic Management and Organisational Dynamics, R.D. Stacey (Pitman 2nd Edition 1996). A thorough analysis of conventional and more recent understandings of how organizations change.

Change: Principles of Problem Formation and Problem Resolution, P. Watzlawick, J. Weakland and R. Fisch (Norton 1974). A seminal work which has influenced current thinking in training therapy and consulting.

Strategies for Managing Change, W.G. Dyer (Addison-Wesley 1984). A straightforward guide to planned change with a useful matrix of possible interventions.

'Managing the Human Side of Change', R. Moss Kanter, *Management Review*, April 1985. Contains a useful analysis of the reasons managers resist change.

Visualizing Change: Model Building and the Change Process, G. Lippitt (University Associates 1973). A rigorous classification and description of change models; how to use them and construct them.

Images of Organization, G. Morgan (Sage 1997). An inspiring book which describes different ways of conceptualizing about organizations.

Organizational Culture and Leadership, E. Schein (Jossey-Bass 1985). An elegant and comprehensive blend of theory and research.

Systems Behaviour, Open Systems Group (ed.) (Harper and Row 1985). An Open University set book on open systems theory and its applications.

The Essence of Strategic Management, C. Bowman (Prentice Hall 1990); *Strategic Thinking*, G. Pearson (Prentice Hall 1990). These two books provide a basic introduction to organizational strategy.

Charting the Corporate Mind, C. Hampden-Turner (Blackwell 1990). The theory and practice of organizational consulting. It offers practical tips as well as broad-ranging concepts.

Leaders, Fools and Imposters, M. Kets de Vries (Jossey-Bass 1993). An examination of how the personality and personal history of the leader can affect organizational success.

Of the titles listed below, the first four are classic OD texts:

Process Consultation: Its Role in Organization Development, (Vols I and II) E. Schein (Addison-Wesley 1988 and 1989).

Organization Development: its Nature, Origins and Prospects, W.G. Bennis (Addison-Wesley 1969).

Developing Organizations: Diagnosis and Action, P.R. Lawrence and J.W. Lorsch (Addison-Wesley 1969).

Organization Development: Strategies and Models, R. Beckhard
(Addison-Wesley 1969).

Career Dynamics: Matching Individual and Organization Needs, E.
Schein (Addison-Wesley 1978). Describes the organizational
implications of life and career changes.
Managing with People: a Manager's Handbook, J.K. Fordyce and R.
Weil (Addison-Wesley 1983). A good overview of OD
methods, emphasizing collaboration between managers and
OD specialists.

Index

Page numbers in italics refer to figures or diagrams related to the topic.

227

Choosing and Using Training Consultants

Diane Bailey and Clare Sproston

As the need for training continues to grow, many organizations are finding that they can no longer fulfil all the demands for training from their own resources. More and more therefore they are turning to specialist consultants for help. Personnel and training managers and others involved are having to develop the skills of working with consultants, many of whom are themselves new to the business. The present book has been produced to answer precisely two key questions: how to chooose a consultant and how to ensure the maximum benefit to the organization. It is based on the authors' own experience of working as consultants with a wide variety of clients. They provide a step-by-step guide designed to achieve a relationship that is as productive as possible. Among the topics covered are:

• preparing the ground • finding and selecting a consultant
• preparing a brief • considering the proposal • contracting
• managing the project • managing the consultant
• evaluating results.

The book also functions as a working document. By completing the instruments, charts and activities it contains the reader can develop a personal reference and action manual. For anyone contemplating the use of consultants for training this book is the most helpful starting point imaginable.

Gower

Designing Training Programmes

Dick Leatherman

You've carried out a training needs analysis and listed the topics your programme should cover. Now how do you set about determining the content? Or identifying the most appropriate teaching methods?

Dick Leatherman's book sets out a ten-step process for developing training programmes tailored to your own requirements. Based on a coherent set of learning principles, it guides you through each of the activities involved, from formulating objectives to designing the post-course evaluation. Additional sections provide expert advice on reviewing off-the-shelf training packages and choosing, and working with, outside consultants.

For trainers and others seeking a simple, systematic approach to the design of programmes Dr Leatherman's book would be hard to better.

Gower

Evaluating Management Development, Training and Education

Second Edition

Mark Easterby-Smith

This ambitious book offers a comprehensive guide to evaluation as applied to management development. It deals in detail with the technical aspects of evaluation, but its main value probably lies in its treatment of more subtle and possibly more important questions such as the politics of using evaluations, the range of purposes to which they may be put, and the effect of different contexts on evaluation practice.

The second edition reflects the many changes that have taken place in the world of management since the original text was compiled, in particular the Management Charter Initiative and the move towards competence-based training. The text has been updated throughout, and many new examples and case studies have been added, including a number from Europe and North America.

For anyone concerned with management development, whether as teacher, trainer or consultant, Dr Easterby-Smith's text will be indispensable.

Gower

Gower Handbook of Training and Development

Second Edition

Edited by John Prior

This Gower Handbook, published in association with the Institute of Training and Development, first appeared in 1991 and quickly established itself as a standard work. For this new edition the text has been completely revised to reflect recent developments and new chapters have been added on cultural diversity, learning styles and choosing resources. The *Handbook* now contains contributions from no fewer than forty-nine experienced professionals, each one an expert in his or her chosen subject.

For anyone involved in training and development, whether in business or the public sector, the *Handbook* represents an unrivalled resource.

Gower

A Handbook for Training Strategy

Martyn Sloman

The traditional approach to training in the organization is no longer effective. That is the central theme of Martyn Sloman's challenging book. A new model is required that will reflect the complexity of organizational life, changes in the HR function and the need to involve line management. This *Handbook* introduces such a model and describes the practical implications not only for human resource professionals and training managers but also for line managers.

Martyn Sloman writes as an experienced training manager and his book is concerned above all with implementation. Thus his text is supported by numerous questionnaires, survey instruments and specimen documents. It also contains the findings of an illuminating survey of best training practice carried out among UK National Training Award winners.

The book is destined to make a significant impact on the current debate about how to improve organizational performance. With its thought-provoking argument and practical guidance it will be welcomed by everyone with an interest in the business of training and development.

Gower

Handbook of
Technology-Based Training

Edited by Brian Tucker
The Forum for Technology in Training

Technology-based training (TBT) has moved a long way since the
early days of computer-based training in the 1960s and 1970s.
Today it offers a flexible, cost-effective way of meeting the ever
increasing need for people to re-skill.

Handbook of Technology-Based Training provides an accessible
guide to the potential benefits and pitfalls of this form of training.
It describes the evolution of technology-based training; the various
technologies and their uses; the benefits of using such flexible
learning; the important issues of how to use the technology; how to
implement TBT in an organization and where the future might lie.
Brian Tucker also deals with choosing and evaluating generic
training and the issues of bespoke training, either produced
in-house or outsourced.

The *Handbook* is not highly technical, and deals with the issues in
a readily understandable way. It uses examples and detailed case
studies to demonstrate how nine leading organizations have
managed the various issues and how they have benefited from this
approach to training. These include Sun Life, Vauxhall, Lloyds Bank,
Argos, British Gas and British Steel.

Structured in two parts, the first provides a complete overview of
the subject. The second consists of a directory of over 700 generic
TBT courseware titles, indexed by subject, title, medium, and
producer. Each entry includes the title of the courseware, its
purpose and suitability, a brief description, delivery methods,
hardware requirements, price and supplier details.

Gower

How to Deliver Training

Martin Orridge

'The aim of this book is to provide both managers wishing to run 'in team' exercises and those entering the training profession with a practical guide to delivering successful developmental events', says Martin Orridge in the Preface.

He writes as an experienced trainer and consultant, producing a very human guide to the realities of running a training event. In a brief introductory section he explains the need for training and the benefits it can bring. Part 1 of the main text shows how to design a successful training session and Part 2 deals in detail with preparation and delivery. At the end is a collection of model documents and forms that can be used at various stages of the training cycle. The text includes tips, tools, checklists, examples and exercises throughout, together with real-life anecdotal 'cameos' to help make the points memorable.

Martin Orridge's style is at all times practical and friendly. *How To Deliver Training* will be welcomed not only by professional trainers, but by all managers and team leaders concerned with staff development.

Gower

How to Measure Training Effectiveness

Third Edition

Leslie Rae

This is a revised and enlarged edition of an outstandingly successful book. In it, Leslie Rae describes a variety of ways in which training can be assessed for effectiveness and value. He covers the entire training process from selecting and planning a training event to validating and testing its outcome. Most of the techniques presented can be applied equally to single events and to a complete programme.

New to the Third Edition:

- existing material (nine chapters) brought fully up to date
- three entirely new chapters on the evaluation process added
- details of the latest competence standards produced by the Training and Development Lead Body.

The book is designed as a practical guide and is written in non-technical language. It will be particularly helpful to newly appointed trainers and to line managers with training responsibility.

Gower

Managerial Consulting Skills

A Practical Guide

Charles J Margerison

The advisory role in organizations is more important today than it has ever been. To perform effectively, managers and professionals need the skills of the consultant.

This book has been designed to provide practical help for all advisers, whether working within or outside the organization. It covers every aspect of the process from interpersonal skills to organizational context, from planning to follow-up. Each chapter concludes with guidelines summarizing the content, and questions designed to help the reader to apply the material to his or her own activities. Fascinating real-life cases from Professor Margerison's own experience are included, as well as examples drawn from the work of many well-known consultants.

Gower

Participative Training Skills

John Rodwell

It is generally accepted that, for developing skills, participative methods are the best. Here at last is a practical guide to maximizing their effectiveness.

Drawing on his extensive experience as a trainer, John Rodwell explores the whole range of participative activities from the trainer's point of view. The first part of his book looks at the principles and the 'core skills' involved. It shows how trainee participation corresponds to the processes of adult learning and goes on to describe each specific skill, including the relevant psychological models. The second part devotes a chapter to each method, explaining:

- what it is
- why and when it is used
- how to apply the core skills in relation to the method
- how to deal with potential problems.

A 'skills checklist' summarizes the guidelines presented in the chapter. The book ends with a comprehensive matrix showing which method is most suitable for meeting which objectives.

For anyone concerned with skill development *Participative Training Skills* represents an invaluable handbook.

Gower

Planning and Designing Training Programmes

Leslie Rae

The quality of the planning will be instrumental to the ultimate success of any training or development programme, yet as the demands on today's trainers are constantly changing, the pressure to devise effective training, often at short notice, is increasing.

This book by one of the UK's leading training authors looks in detail at the entire planning process, set very much within today's challenging corporate context. Following the book will enable any trainer to devise a professional training and development programme, by:

• identifying and analysing training needs
• designing and planning a programme to meet them
• designing and planning the individual sessions within it
• evaluating success - at the start, during, and at the end of the programme.

Included are all the considerations a trainer needs to be aware of, ranging from skills assessment and learning styles, to relative benefits of on the job and off the job training, and the value of different types of training formats. Finding time for proper evaluation is crucial too, and Leslie Rae highlights a wide range of options. Also included is a unique index of available training resources.

This exceptionally practical structured approach will help any trainer to shorten the planning time involved whilst improving the quality of that preparation.

Gower

Running an Effective Training Session

Patrick Forsyth

This down-to-earth guide to planning and delivering a training session will be welcomed by new and experienced trainers alike - as well as by line managers and other professionals with training responsibility. In this book Patrick Forsyth takes the reader step by step through the process of structuring the session and preparing materials, before covering the presentational techniques involved in detail. The final section is concerned with following up in terms of evaluation and establishing links to further training. The user-friendly text is supported throughout by examples.

For anyone involved in training, Patrick Forsyth's book represents a painless way to improve performance.

Gower

75 Ways to Liven Up Your Training

A Collection of Energizing Activities

Martin Orridge

Most of the activities in Martin Orridge's book require little in the way of either expertise or equipment. Yet they provide a powerful way of stimulating creativity, helping people to enjoy learning, or simply injecting new momentum into the training process.

Each activity is presented under a standard set of headings, including a brief description, a statement of purpose, likely duration, a note of any materials required and detailed instructions for running the event. In addition there are suggestions for debriefing and possible variations.

To help users to select the most appropriate activities they are arranged in the book by type or process. There are exercises for individuals, pairs and large groups and they range from icebreakers to closing events.

Trainers, managers, team leaders and anyone responsible for developing people will find this volume a rich store-house of ideas.

Gower